A concise and useful analysis of the legal landscape facing both cloud providers and their customers

Cloud Computing

Security Compliance and Governance

What's the risk..................................
legal Challenges.................................
T&C's for Cloud Contracts......................
Information ownership in the cloud............
Data Protection and Accountability...........
Technical Challenges...........................
Trust, Cloud Governance and Standards...
Use of Security Standards.....................
Process and Control............................
Understanding the Division of Liability......
Compliance and Audit...........................
Reasonable Security in the Cloud.............
Essential Contractual Clauses.................

.................and much more

Russell Ballantine

Cloud Computing,

Security Compliance and Governance

R.Ballantine CISSP, LLM, BSc (hons)

Acknowledgments

I would like to thank Jeremy Warner of Strathclyde University for providing valuable guidance during the completion of this work. Also my current employer Cable and Wireless. From within C&W I am grateful to the following colleagues for valuable information on a particular approach to cloud computing: Howard Blindell (Senior Network and Security Engineer, C&W), Jim Reynolds (Data Network Design Engineer, C&W), Jim Credland (Head of Information Assurance, Governance, Risk and Regulatory Affairs) and Alex Lindle (Information Assurance, Governance, Risk and Regulatory Affairs.) I also extend my gratitude to Alan Hazzard (European Patent Attorney, Pilkington Plc) for his invaluable assistance on some peripheral issues of intellectual property.

Finally, my family for giving me time and support.

Errors or omissions are all due to the author.

Table of Contents

Chapter One

Cloud

Computing

ChapterTwo

Information

Security

Chapter Three

Corporate Dilligence and
Compliance

Chapter Four: *Putting it all together*

Table of Cases

W Abel and B Schafer, "The German Constitutional Court on the Right in Confidentiality and

Abbreviations

NIST	National Institute of Standards and Technology
OCC	Open Cloud Consortium
UCTA	Unfair Contract Terms Act
CCMF	The Cloud Computing Manifesto
API	Application Program Interface
SLA	Service Level Agreement
CC-BoR	Cloud Computing Bill of Rights
CSP	Cloud Service Provider
CAMM	Common Assurance Maturity Model
ICT	Information and Communication Technology
ITU	International Telecommunication Union
ToS	Terms of Service (the cloud service contract)
ENISA	European Network and Information Security Agency
DMTF	Distributed Management Task Force
DMCA	Digital Millenium and Copyright Act
OECD	Organization for Economic Co-operation and Development
PABX	Private Automatic Branch Exchange
UN	United Nations
EU	European Union
WSIS	World Summit on the Information Society
GLB	Gramm–Leach–Bliley
CSA	Cloud Security Alliance

Introduction

Internet and computer related crime is a growing challenge. Every computer journal, legal journal, IT magazine or techy blog tells us this and they are filled with useful information to help the budding CSO bolster his defences. That's Chief Security Officer (CSO)[1] that most important of posts giving board level representation for all security related matters. The starting point for a 'top down' approach to corporate security which ensures sound governance frameworks are built on solid foundations with all responsibility and accountability clearly visible for all to see, even your auditors.........

Wake up, the fact that most organisations don't actually employ a dedicated CSO[2] should tell us something about the reality of the situation. A cynical analysis might ascertain that the 'compliance industry' is playing the market, plying its latest must have snake oil products and consultancy services to ensure you are forewarned and prepared for............well prepared for what exactly?

Cloud computing could change everything. The current case of ***Google v. The United States*** involving two giants of the Internet service market illustrates the potential for conflict within this emerging market.[3] Just what exactly cloud computing is we look at below in the first chapter of this book but for the moment it suffices to mention one important point. A company utilising cloud services will, in a lot of cases, be moving data processing capabilities and sensitive data outside of its own corporate firewall infrastructure. Traditionally the firewall has marked not just a technological boundary but also a demarcation point for information security responsibilities. For cloud computing to be successful[4] a lot of issues relating to data protection, privacy, intellectual property and trust will need to be successfully addressed. This is nothing new these issues have

---

[1] http://en.wikipedia.org/wiki/Chief_security_officer

[2] Advisory services, Trial by Fire – finding 6. http://download.pwc.com/ie/pubs/trial_by_fire.pdf
The CSO role in a lot of organisations is lumped in with the CEO role or some other role. In a lot of cases the 'security umbrella' is itself umbrella'd under an IT function.

[3] The American Department of Industry selected Microsoft to deliver a 'private cloud' for delivery of consolidated messaging services. Google are claiming anti competitive behavior and arguing the insistence on a private cloud is not necessary and illustrative of a pre-determined decision by the government. NB The terms private and public when applied to a cloud architecture are explained later in this document.

[4] A lot of major companies are already building their cloud infrastructures in order to be ahead of the game. All the major telecoms companies, ISP's and other Internet based companies, who suddenly find they are well positioned to provide cloud services for customers are already creating demand by showing the cost effectiveness of the cloud solution.

been around for a while. The difference now is that clarification of the legal position and the setting up of an effective governance framework for 'the cloud' is becoming a business driver for the take up of cloud services. A company's liability for data protection and information privacy when using a cloud service will not change. Cloud providers will need to persuade their customers and specifically their legal and regulatory and assurance departments that they can be trusted with their data. Trusted with their liability!! This is trust on a whole new level. This **IS** new.

The dichotomy between ownership and control and of responsibility and accountability for data protection and information security raises important questions which, once answered, will define a minimum standard of care that may become an adequacy baseline below which corporations may face criminal or civil liability. These questions are:

1. What responsibility does an organisation have for protecting information belonging to its self and others which resides on its computer systems?

2. What responsibility does that organisation have for ensuring its computer systems and the information they contain is not used to harm others?

Answering these questions will require clarity to be brought to difficult areas of developing law such as:

- The evolving legislative landscape involving the duty of information holders to protect information belonging to others.

- The law of contract when relating to issues of information protection.

- The developing best practice guidelines of industry standards regarding information security.

The legal and compliance challenges raised by the above questions will affect the level of trust a client can put in a provider. To develop that trust a cloud provider must be transparent about its cloud platforms risk exposure and its own mitigation plans for handling that risk. From the providers point of view failure to follow industry best practice with regards to information security or a lack of understanding of the issues involved will undermine the organisations ability to limit it's liability via express contractual clauses for information and other security breaches. Severe mishandling of these issues could even result in negligence claims. On the other hand a corporate customer wishing to make use of cloud services from a cloud provider must, via his own diligence, assess prudently the risk associated with using the service. The responsibility for ensuring that a particular cloud service is fit for purpose must be taken seriously.

This analysis, divided into four chapters, studies the problems of data protection and information security arising as businesses (both service providers and consumers) move to benefit from cloud computing. The current framework of legislation and regulation for information security enforces no specific security model but does create an obligation for *reasonable security measures*' to be in place to protect information assets. This booklet will attempt to outline an approach to information security governance which will allow organisations to achieve legal compliance whilst utilising cloud computing in its business model.

Chapter one *attempts* to define cloud computing and how it differs from other computing models. It looks at the difficulties in managing it and provides a preliminary discussion of the legal challenges created. **Chapter two** examines what is meant by information security and what 'reasonable security' means in a cloud computing context particularly with regards to data protection. It also re-visits, in greater detail, some of the legal problems outlined in chapter one and discusses how an organisation can behave reasonably in the eyes of the law to address some of the issues. **Chapter three** looks at corporate diligence and compliance from an information security point of view and assesses the importance of certain elements of governance in creating and maintaining a reasonable corporate security footprint. And finally **chapter four** pulls together our assessment of what is wrong with the current position and puts forward suggestions for moving towards a compliance landscape that allows cloud computing, data protection and information privacy to coexist. It discusses how at the present time reasonable security must be maintained through contract law and examines proposed contractual provisions

Chapter One

Cloud Computing

"...the phrase du jour"

1.1   What is Cloud Computing?

The term 'cloud computing' is indeed the latest buzzword to permeate the journals and newsletters of the IT and telecommunications industry. The 'cloud' cliché has been used to represent the nebulous character of the Internet for quite some time and it should come as no surprise that when combined with the word computing 'cloud computing' equally defies clear definition. There are as many 'definitions' as there are companies queuing up to offer cloud computing services to industry and the public. Cloud computing is slowly transforming itself from hype to reality. The uptake of any cloud service is dependant on the vendor's abilities to address potential customers concerns as: security in the cloud, interoperability and portability of vendor services, and governance of the service infrastructure. In the world of Internet technology windows of opportunity never stay open for long. A vendor's best chance of addressing these concerns is adherence to industry guidelines and standards.[5] With an irony worthy of Catch-22[6] a definition of cloud computing is a key requirement to setting up a standards based framework for its governance. To that end NIST has developed the following working definition:

> "Cloud computing is a model for enabling convenient, on-demand
> network access to a shared pool of configurable computing
> resources (e.g., networks, servers, storage, applications, and
> services) that can be rapidly provisioned and released with minimal
> management effort or service provider interaction. This
> cloud model promotes availability and is composed of five
> essential characteristics, three delivery models, and four deployment models.[7] "

This definition will suffice for our purposes. The 'essential characteristics' of this model will be discussed in the next section (1.1.2) where we clarify the terminology used when discussing cloud computing.

Cloud computing networks, usually housed in traditional data centres, are large groups of servers often using virtualization techniques[8] to provide a rapidly scalable resource pool which can be utilised to deliver computing resources as an 'on demand' service for customers. Of fundamental interest to our analysis is how the cloud computing paradigm influences the corporate perimeter for

---

[5] http://www.mel.nist.gov/div826/msid/sima/interopweek/presentations/openStdsinFed_IT.pdf : Role of Open Standards in IT and Telecommunications. Mary Mitchel, March 2006
[6] The famous satirical novel by Joseph Heller.
[7] Draft Working Definition of Cloud Computing V14, US National Institute of Standards, June 2009
[8] http://searchservervirtualization.techtarget.com/sDefinition/0,,sid94_gci499539,00.html

vendor and customer interaction. Certain responsibilities, as we shall see, cannot be outsourced.

1.1.2 A Glossary of Terms

A discussion of cloud computing involves some new terminology which may not be familiar to the reader. Although not comprehensive the following provides some guidance.

Public and Private clouds: Corporate perimeters are usually defined using firewall technology. Over the years this perimeter has become more and more porous[9] until today with the advent of cloud computing corporate services are actually placed outside the firewall on a public cloud utilising shared architecture and shared resources with other corporate entities (***Multi-Tenant***). Private clouds may be used for more sensitive data types where the cloud environment is still created using shared infrastructure and resources but at a companies own datacenter behind its own firewall perimeter. The concept of perimeter is not just a technological issue but also one of corporate responsibility and has implications for an organisations due diligence (see Chpt's 3, 4). Private clouds allow the removal of a number of common objections to the cloud computing model involving: security, customer data handling and regulatory compliance.

Cloud Apps: The application running in the cloud is never installed on the local computer. With broadband speeds increasing and dependable connectivity it is now practical to run applications from afar with the overhead on disk storage, cpu and memory usage etc borne by the hosting provider. Most current cloud providers create a development environment where users can create their own apps and even make money from them.[10]Common cloud apps currently in use are: Gmail, Picnik, WordPress, Zoho Office Suite etc[11]. This would constitute what is known as a ***SaaS*** (Software as a Service) delivery.

PaaS: '*Platform as a Service*' has evolved to run the custom 'cloud apps' mentioned above. Organisations such as SalesForce[12] offer all the resources needed to develop and run applications over the Internet. These resources are delivered as a utility service similar to electricity or water where users 'tap in' take and pay for what they need. Billing is via a metering or a subscription model offered by the cloud provider.

IaaS: Finally Infrastructure as a Service, the third layer,[13]describes the provisioning model for computer infrastructure such as virtualized hardware being delivered as a service. Software and servers are purchased as a fully outsourced resource and billing takes into account how much of

---

[9] Beyond Borders: Losing the perimeter to gain better data security, Anne Saita 'SearchSecurity.com' 2004
[10] Windows Azure: www.microsoft.com/uk/net , Android phone apps: http://developer.android.com/index.html
[11] http://dvice.com/archives/2008/10/top-10-cloud-ap.php
[12] http://www.salesforce.com/paas/
[13] From Sun Microsystems white paper on cloud architecture. '***Introduction to Cloud Computing Architecture***' http://whitepapers.techrepublic.com.com/abstract.aspx?docid=1188419

the resource is actually used. This is usually referred to as the cloud providers '*enterprise hosting platform.*'

Cloud Provider: The service provider that offers customers storage, infrastructure or software services, usually via the Internet, is known as the cloud provider. They will own or lease large datacenter spaces and run suites of virtualised servers which can be configured to provide public or private cloud environments. Online data management/storage services can be utilised which allow organisations to store data on the Internet (*Cloud Storage*). This will, by design, be outside the organisations firewall perimeter (public cloud) or inside (private cloud). How particular data types are handled in these public or private environments will be of particular interest us. Issues of data protection, regulatory compliance and to a lesser degree intellectual property will feature prominently in the analysis.

1.2 Legal Challenges

Corporations are developing cloud platforms at breakneck speed, rushing to realise the potential for capital gain and cost reduction inherent in the cloud computing approach.[14] The legal framework for cloud although developing at a much slower pace will need to incorporate change quicker than it has traditionally done so. The concept of security encompasses legal provision and obligation that must be evaluated in any cloud computing deployment. Laws such as the *US export controls* and the *UK Data Protection Act* may change significantly in the long term but for business purposes the short term implications of them on PaaS and SaaS architectures make the public cloud a nefarious environment. For a particular business purpose it may be easier to manage your organisations data handling obligations in a private cloud. Corporations will need to understand subtle distinctions which may have not so subtle implications on their responsibilities.

When a client uses a cloud service he passes in some capacity (dependant on the service detail) control to the provider which obviously affects the security posture of the client. The hope is that good governance will ensure this is a good thing. However it is, as we shall see, very easy for a gap in governance to result. If a service level agreement (SLA) or a contract does not commit the provider to maintaining all the client's security obligations the client must be careful to ensure these obligations are met via other means such as stringent audit of the provider's process control and infrastructure. The client must also be aware that cloud computing is not just a new more efficient way of outsourcing.[15] Using a cloud service may expose the client to new governance issues which

---

[14] http://www.the-financedirector.com/features/feature61743/ : The Financial Benefits of Cloud Computing, John Lees. CFO Star Assure

[15] There is much debate as to the relationship between cloud computing and outsourcing with some authors maintaining there is no difference. This author believes the argument to be irrelevant and cloud computing is best

can create liability for him. The law does not allow all responsibilities to be outsourced and clients must be aware and prepared when these governance gaps develop as a result of moving to a cloud service delivery.

1.2.1 Terms and Conditions for Cloud Computing Contracts

Specific issues associated with cloud computing arise in the areas of law associated with privacy, data transfer, intellectual property, third-party access and consumer rights etc. We are concerned in this analysis with how the legal concept of 'reasonable security' is to be maintained and what effect it will have on implied terms within cloud computing contracts. During the research phase of this booklet the intention was to use survey material from service providers in the form of a questionnaire this proved to be a difficult and un-rewarding pursuit.[16] The endeavour undertaken even with my own employer led me to conclude that this result is in no small part due to the lack of maturity of most organisations governance frameworks for their cloud hosting platforms. Service providers are in a 'gold rush' phase at present where the need to build and get something out there takes precedent over too rigorous an approach to diligence. In order to reap the rewards providers are leaving the unanswered questions of security and liability to another day and treating this as an acceptable risk.

However other better placed organisations with more industry influence than me have been more successful in their attempts to survey cloud providers for information and I have made use of their findings to illustrate points where required.[17]

Most commercial cloud service providers make available their standard contract terms on their web pages so that potential customers can review and compare T&C's. The documentation making up the T&C's can be short and simple or long and wieldy but generally a cloud consumer[18] 'contract' is made up from the following.[19]

Terms of Service (ToS) document the relationship between the provider and customer. They contain any legal clauses and disclaimers and reference any other T&C documents.

---

thought of as a new mechanism or model to perform outsourcing.

[16] See Appendix 1 for questionnaire.

[17] For example the Queen Mary University of London (QMUL) Cloud Legal Project has produced useful research relating to cloud provider terms and conditions in contracts and will be quoted in this report in support of findings.

[18] Commercial negotiated contracts are discussed later in this document.

[19] Contracts for Clouds: Comparison and Analysis of the Terms and Conditions of Cloud Computing Services: Queen Mary University of London, School of Law Legal Studies Research Paper No. 63/2010. (Page 14).

Service Level Agreement (SLA) for any paid for aspects of the service this document details the level of service to be delivered and the compensation process in event of service failure.

Acceptable Use Policy (AUP) usually documents what you cannot do with the service.

Privacy Policy Details how the provider will protect (and use) your personal information in accordance with privacy and data protection laws.

1.2.2 Contract Formation

At one level of abstraction there are only two categories of contract depending on whether the provider is offering a free service or a paid one. However with regards to information a provider may extract a non-monitory cost from the consumer for a 'free' service. Through license terms the provider may seek to re-use customer data for its own purposes. For example the following license term is imposed by Apple for material uploaded to its iWorks application[20]:

"5. Content Submitted or Made Available by You on the Service

License from You

Except for material we may license to you, Apple does not claim ownership of the materials and/or Content you submit or make available on the Service. However, by submitting or posting such Content on areas of the Service that are accessible by the public, you grant Apple a worldwide, royalty-free, non-exclusive license to use, distribute, reproduce, modify, adapt, publish, translate, publicly perform and publicly display such Content on the Service solely for the purpose for which such Content was submitted or made available. Said license will terminate within a commercially reasonable time after you or Apple remove such Content from the public area. By submitting or posting such Content on areas of the Service that are accessible by the public, you are representing that you are the owner of such material and/or have authorization to distribute it."

Social networking companies such as Facebook offer facilities to host user content and web services on behalf of users so can also be considered as offering free cloud services.[21] Contracts involving paid for services vary between those which use the standard-form contract of the provider and those which are fully negotiated depending on relative bargaining positions of the provider and customer.

For free services supplied via the Internet it may be questionable whether an enforceable contract is actually ever formed. For example in English law there may not be sufficient 'consideration' present to form a contract. In these cases a conditional license agreement

---

[20] Extract from Apple iWorks Terms of Use Agreement http://www.apple.com/legal/iworkcom/en/terms.html
[21] See Article: Facebook's New Terms Of Service: "We Can Do Anything We Want With Your Content. Forever." By Chris Walters for a discussion on their T&Cs

may still be deemed operable where the provider is offering a free service in return for the customer abiding by the providers terms. In Europe consumers are to a great degree protected from unreasonable contract terms and to a lesser degree businesses are also protected from particularly harsh terms[22]. In this document we will be mainly concerned with commercial negotiated cloud contracts and the effectiveness of contractual terms in both protecting customer data and clarifying provider obligation for such. In the final chapter (chapter 4) 'putting it all together' we will look at effective and fair contract formation that recognises the obligations created through law as well as the reasonableness of the expectations placed on both the provider and customer.

1.2.3 Jurisdiction and Applicable Law

The 30th Council of Europe Conference of Ministers of Justice met in Istanbul on 24th November this year (2010)[23]. Discussions involving the issues arising as a result of cloud computing infused very much the substance of 'Resolution No.3, on data protection and privacy in the third millennium'. After reiterating, in paragraph 4, the importance of privacy as a fundamental human right[24] and the threat it faces from modern communication technology, paragraph 6 specifically mentions the challenges introduced to information security by cloud computing.[25]

The T&C of most cloud providers will attempt to assert the applicable law which will govern the contract. International operators may specify differing legal systems dependent on the location of the customer.[26] However individual cloud customers in some jurisdictions may be protected by consumer protection laws from contract terms which try to enforce a foreign

---

[22] **Kingsway Hall Hotel v Red Sky IT (Houslow) [2010] EWHC 965 (TCC) HHJ**. – Specialist knowledge and expertise of a provider creates obligations for the provider during contract formation. They must not exploit the customer's lack of expertise to secure unfair contract terms.

[23] http://www.coe.int/t/dghl/standardsetting/minjust/mju30/MJU-30%20_2010_%20RESOL%203%20E%20final.pdf

[24] "4. Noting that modern information and communication technologies (hereafter "ICTs") enable observation, storage and analysis of most day-to-day human activities, more easily, rapidly and invisibly than ever before, thereby potentially creating a feeling of being permanently watched, which may impair the free exercise of human rights and fundamental freedoms unless robust standards of data protection are effectively enforced worldwide;"

[25] "6. Noting with concern the challenges to the enforcement of data protection principles resulting from unresolved issues of jurisdiction and applicable law in respect of virtual and trans border relationships (e.g. cloud-computing tools, social networks);"

[26] "…….ONLY THE LIMITATIONS WHICH ARE LAWFUL IN YOUR JURISDICTION WILL APPLY TO YOU AND OUR LIABILITY WILL BE LIMITED TO THE MAXIMUM EXTENT PERMITTED BY LAW." – Excerpt from Google's terms of service on warranty exclusions. http://www.google.com/accounts/TOS

legal system on them. As well as jurisdiction the cloud contract may try to impose a relatively short claim period in respect of the service. For example Rackspace requires claims to be brought within 2 years.[27] Again customers within the EEA may have some protection against these limitation periods.[28]

For cloud computing questions of jurisdiction and applicable law will necessarily involve questions of information ownership and trust. Ownership in an information sense raises legal questions of personal property which are largely outside the scope of this analysis.[29] However we are very interested in the obligation of confidence owed to the consumer or customer by the provider for information placed in a cloud environment. The nature of cloud computing relationships requires an element of trust and an information owners right's of confidentiality (express or implied) should not be affected simply by putting information in the cloud. A lot of the information exchanged or carried in the cloud will be confidential in nature. Information uploaded to the provider by the cloud service consumer will carry with it an expectation of maintained confidentiality or security at least as good as that available to the consumer on his own network.[30] However this 'confidential relationship' is best maintained and clarified through a contractual term to avoid misunderstandings. Once information becomes known outside of a confidential environment there is case law to say that the protection is lost.[31] The question of information ownership and confidentiality is examined fuller in the next section (1.2.4).

From a privacy and data protection perspective the main law in Europe is developed from 'EU Directive 95/46/EC' which was initially developed in the pre-Internet era when processing facilities were more severely limited than now. Cloud computing exposes the age and complexity of the current laws[32] and severe problems arise for the concept of processing. Both the cloud provider and the customer share the processing means. The European legislation makes a statutory assumption that the controller is solely in control of all processing. In cloud computing it can be argued that this is not always the case. Data processing 'equipment' becomes extremely hard to define but can be crucial to determining jurisdiction and applicable law. The definition could range from processing in an EU based data centre to a cookie hosted

---

[27] http://www.rackspacecloud.com/legal/ (paragraph 28).

[28] See sub-paragraph (q) of Council Directive 93/13/EEC (Annex) on Unfair Terms in Consumer Contracts.

[29] For a fairly detailed analysis of ownership issues for digital information in the cloud see "Information 'ownership' in the cloud" by Chris Reed, CCLS Legal Aspects of Cloud Computing Research Project. Research paper No. 45/2010 Queen Mary University of London.

[30] See e.g. Saltman Engineering v Campbell (1948) 65 RPC 203

[31] See e.g. Attorney-General v Guardian Newspapers Ltd [1990] 1 AC 109

[32] For instance for data protection: who is the controller? , what law is applicable? And other relevant law may be less restrictive in application e.g. US approach to privacy.

in a browser on a computer in the EU. Even the use of virtual rooms and video conferencing facilities can create problems (see ***Forward Foods LLC v. Next Proteins)***[33]

1.2.4   Information Ownership in the Cloud

A legal analysis of information ownership in a cloud context is not an easy task because information has a fluid dynamic constantly being added to, modified and removed at any moment in time. A number of different areas of law (such as property law, law of confidence, data protection and contract law) come together to create expectations which are fundamental to cloud computing relationships. However, although difficult, an analysis of information ownership in a cloud computing context needs to be undertaken if we are to understand how a legal expectation of reasonable security will affect implied liabilities and contract terms.

Cloud relationships can be complicated and involve a number of different participants. For instance in any cloud service the service provider may make use of third party companies to provide parts of that cloud service. In fact the cloud framework and the terms of service may even make it clear that information processing will be performed by third party companies as part of the providers cloud service.[34] These relationships will be controlled via contract but it is a complicating factor that needs to be taken into consideration by any business customer seeking to utilise cloud services from a provider. Unfortunately there also exists some worrying case law such as ***United States v. Miller***[35] which suggests personal data sourced from a third party (such as an individual's bank) is not subject to the same controls as that data sourced from the individual.

For the purposes of our analysis we can consider two primary information channels.

- Information generated outside the cloud (usually by the customer then placed on cloud)

- Information generated inside the cloud (by customer or provider)

---

[33] Forward Foods LLC v. Next Proteins, Inc, 873 N.Y.S.2d 511, 2008 WL 4602345 N.Y. The court in this case held that use of virtual rooms to share documentation can serve as a "contact" for personal jurisdiction purposes.
[34] Google terms of service para 4.1, http://www.google.com/accounts/TOS

[35] "the case stands generally for the proposition that an individual's personal records held by a third party does not have the same constitutional privacy protection as applies to the same record held by the individual" - http://www.worldprivacyforum.org/pdf/WPF_Cloud_Privacy_Report.pdf

An enterprise corporation utilising a cloud service will for a large part of its business generate information outside the cloud environment (within its own infrastructure) and then place that information in the cloud to make use of the cloud service for further processing. The information therefore has an established ownership before it goes into the cloud. It is reasonable to assume that the mere act of placing the information on the cloud will not change this.[36] The law relating to the protection of confidential information or trade secrets is important here to our discussion on ownership rights. Art. 39(2) of the Agreement on Trade-Related Aspects of Intellectual Property Rights (TRIPS Agreement)[37] states:

---

2. Natural and legal persons shall have the possibility of preventing information lawfully within their control from being disclosed to, acquired by, or used by others without their consent in a manner contrary to honest commercial practices so long as such information:

(a) is secret in the sense that it is not, as a body or in the precise configuration and assembly of its components, generally known among or readily accessible to persons within the circles that normally deal with the kind of information in question;

(b) has commercial value because it is secret; and

(c) has been subject to reasonable steps under the circumstances, by the person lawfully in control of the information, to keep it secret.

This forms the consensus of international opinion on the minimum level of protection for confidentiality of commercial information. For non-commercial information there exists an expectation for the protection of confidentiality where an obligation of confidence can be shown to have been assumed.[38] With respect to an individual's privacy rights for information stored on his PC which is subsequently copied to the cloud the case of **State v. Bellar** will have some relevance.[39]

The nature of cloud computing relationships therefore seems to suggest that the cloud service provider has some legal obligation to maintain the confidentiality of the customer's information. Since this expectation seems to already be present in common law[40] it should do no harm for providers to include a confidentiality clause in their ToS. This will also provide an opportunity to clarify limitations on those obligations. For example a service provider may

---

[36] The question of ownership implies some sort of personal property right. The question of property rights for information in a purely digital form is complicated and outside the scope of this document. Also out of scope is discussion of the ownership rights resulting from Intellectual Property and copyright laws which have relevance especially for information contained in databases. In the UK national courts are unlikely to recognise personal property rights in digital information – *St Albans City and District Council v International Computers ltd [1996] 4 All ER 481.*

[37] http://www.wto.org/english/tratop_e/trips_e/t_agm0_e.htm

[38] See Coco v A.N Clark (Engineers) Ltd [1969] RPC 41 and Saltman Engineering v Campbell (1948) 65 RPC 41

[39] "..defendant's privacy rights in the information stored in his personal computer is retained even if the information is copied and stored on a medium owned by someone else." – dissenting opinion of J. Sercombe in *State v. Bellar, 217 P.3d 1094 (Or. App. 2009).*

[40] See note 34 above

receive requests for access to information from law enforcement and how the provider will respond to these requests can be outlined in the service terms.[41] Some CSP T&Cs do in fact contain claims to the effectiveness of their data security practices. However providers need to be careful not to overstate their case here. The recent class action lawsuit ***Gaos v. Google Inc*** shows that a company's T&C claims about data protection will be closely scrutinised by regulators and attorneys.

Ownership and therefore implied obligation for confidentiality of information generated within the cloud environment is more complicated. Through the same reasoning as above we can see that information generated 'in the cloud' by the cloud customer[42] will be protected by the law of confidence in the same way as information generated outside of the cloud. Questions of ownership arising through interpretation of intellectual property law do arise for this information[43] but this is largely out of scope for our purposes here. More interesting for our current analysis is the nature of information generated within the cloud by the cloud provider.

The service provider in the process of running the cloud service will generate information for its own internal purposes such as billing and general network management data. This information is derived from the customer's information and behaviour. Tools are available which can be used to analyse this data and produce yet more useful information for the provider.[44] Two questions immediately spring to mind: what rights does the customer have for controlling the collection and use of this data and are any customer rights infringed by the collection.

If personal data is involved then in the UK the provisions of the Data Protection Act 1998 will need to be adhered to. Other jurisdictions will have there own privacy laws to consider. For the moment we are interested in how the duty of confidentiality owed to the customer by the provider affects the processing of customer information by that provider. Most of the case law which exists to clarify the duty of confidentiality tends to relate to disclosure to other non related third parties[45] and doesn't work to restrict the recipient of the information from utilising it for its

---

[41] Such matters as: whether a court order will be required, how far the customer will be kept informed of developments etc.

[42] Information ownership can be attributed to the customer and therefore an obligation of confidentiality must be assumed.

[43] Mainly in the realm of data base rights for information generated on servers in far flung jurisdictions. For instance European law in this respect differs from that of the US. See Feist Publications Inc. v. Rural Telephone Service Company, Inc. 499 US340 (1990) and compare with the 'sui generic' protection under the Database Directive OJ L77, 27 March 1996 p. 20

[44] Data mining tools generally operate by aggregating data and looking for patterns which provide useful information. However privacy concerns can arise depending on how this is done and the extent of the mining. http://en.wikipedia.org/wiki/Data_mining

[45] For example Seager v Copydex Ltd [1967] 2 All E.R. 415, 417 and for a review of the relevant case law on this point

own business use. At present it does not seem feasible for the customer to rely on obligations of confidentiality to prevent the service provider from engaging in data mining techniques or other information gathering activities. For service providers it would seem a prudent approach to include in the terms of service a clause outlining the processing activities that customer's data will be subjected to both in support of the service provision and for the providers own business uses. If the clause is clear and the customer consents there can be no suggestion of a breach of confidentiality for these mining activities.

The courts seem to be in two minds as to what is necessary to pursue claims for a data breach. If we consider *risk* of identity theft for example as a possible result from a data breech we see in some cases that this is not enough to confer standing[46] whereas in others the opposite proved to be the case.[47] The premise is the need to suffer a direct loss as a result of the breach. In *Ruiz v. Gap* the plaintiff's claim of negligence based on risk of identity theft in the future was dismissed by the court but the judge did note that the plaintiff had standing to assert the claim. However in *Allison v. Aetna* the applicant was deemed to lack standing to pursue negligence and breach of contract because it could not be established that risk of identity theft existed. In both these cases the judge has made an assessment of the likelihood that the breached data will be used to steal identity.

1.2.5 Data Protection, Responsibility and Accountability

Most countries in the world have some form of privacy legislation in place.[48] One of the first tasks facing an organisation moving to a cloud service is identifying relevant privacy legislation for compliance purposes. Not all legislation works in the same way. For example all countries in the European Union are required to develop and implement legislation according to EU Directive 95/46/EC. The emphasis here is data protection with the details of implementation and enforcement left up to the individual member countries. The American approach has a different, sector specific approach to privacy and an emphasis on punitive measures for data breach.[49]

---

see "The (fiduciary) duty of fidelity" [2008] LQR 274 by Robert Flannigan.

[46] E.g. Randolph v. ING Life Ins. And Annuity Co., 486 F.Supp. 2d 1 (D.D.C. 2007)
[47] Caudle v. Towers, Perrin,Forster & Crosby, Inc
[48] (ISC)2 symposium "Legal Issues of the Cloud", Jonathan Armstrong.
[49] http://www.ncsl.org/IssuesResearch/TelecommunicationsInformationTechnology/SecurityBreachNotificationLaws

ENISA is affiliated to the European Union[50] and has produced a useful report "Cloud Computing: Benefits, Risks and Recommendations for Information Security" which outlines both the benefits and pitfalls of the cloud computing model from an information security point of view. This report comments on the lack of clarity within the current regulatory system with regards to cloud computing –

LEGAL RECOMMENDATIONS TO THE EUROPEAN COMMISSION
We recommend that the European Commission study or clarify the following:

⬚ certain issues related to the Data Protection Directive and the recommendations of the Article 29 Data Protection Working Party;

⬚ cloud providers obligation to notify their customers of data security breaches;

- and "*Until legal precedent and regulations address security concerns specific to cloud computing, customers and cloud providers alike should look to the terms of their contract to effectively address security risks.*"

What this means is legal precedent and regulation should not be relied on to ensure data protection in a cloud environment and customers making use of a cloud service should take measures to ensure they meet their compliance obligation in this respect. In European law the cloud customer is the 'data controller' and must check the data handling practices of the cloud provider. Even if contractual terms are formed, creating an obligation on the cloud provider to ensure the customers data privacy needs are met, the customer must check (via effective audit) that this is indeed happening. The cloud customer will be the main party held accountable for the processing of personal information even if that processing is performed by an external third party. Only the physical mechanisms for processing personal data can be handed to another. Responsibility and accountability for correct data processing can not be contracted out. Cloud customers, especially those in the consumer rather than commercial sectors (users of Facebook, Google Apps etc) can easily be unaware of their own responsibilities for data security even when outlined in the service providers ToS. These points will be further expanded in chapter 2: Information Security.

---

[50] ENISA is the European Union's dedicated security agency. The output produced from this agency is likely to be referred to by any regulatory bodies looking for guidance on legal and other issues pertaining to information security and data protection.

1.3   Technical Challenges

Cloud computing is a new way of delivering computing resources. The model has driven technical change such as: concentration of hardware resources in a single area which allows for economies of scale on all aspects of hardware management (datacenter resources) and separation of the physical platform and the service applications (virtualization of the service architecture). The uptake of this model has been rapid with the benefits to cost savings for business obvious. However there are 'new' risks associated with the cloud approach which any business will need to be aware of.

Sharing of resource and multi-tenancy are the key characteristics of cloud computing. Isolation and separation of customer data however must be maintained within this environment while working to preserve the integrity of all data wherever it appears in the cloud. Cloud platforms utilise technology which can be exposed to hacking techniques such as: guest-hopping, SQL Injection and side channel attacks.[51] These attack vectors can make the preservation of data confidentiality challenging. New technical mechanisms separating storage, memory and routing etc should be properly risk assessed for adequacy as part of a cloud providers due diligence. If a cloud provider cannot show adherence to best practice, industry standards or regulatory requirements for the cloud architecture they deploy they put at risk the customers own compliance footprint. For this reason it is important that the cloud customer is able to audit the cloud provider. Only through effective audit can the customer verify the provider is meeting the terms of any contract.

Some of the main technical challenges are set out below.

- *Management interfaces* in public cloud architectures are Internet accessible and although this is nothing new to hosting providers an increased risk is present due to the larger set of resources accessible through these interfaces. These interfaces will typically be accessed using a remote access model or some web based front end both of which present a set of vulnerabilities which needs to be re-evaluated in the cloud context.

- Much is made of the 'plug and play' nature of the *virtualization technology* that underpins

---

[51] For technical details on these hacking techniques see Vulnerability Analysis and Defence for the Internet: Abhishek Singh, Baibhav Singh, Hirosh Joseph, Springer Press.

cloud architectures.[52] For IaaS deliveries the provider will in general take no responsibility for what is done with the virtualised platform. The customer's infrastructure and operations professionals will be expected to manage this burden. These professionals although usually aware of the compliance issues and standards will, in a lot of cases, not be directly involved with the assurance framework. This is very easily one of the places where a governance gap can result for the cloud customer and therefore creates a business risk for both customer and provider.

- IaaS customers are often told of the advantages of using the on demand cloning capabilities of virtual machines to aid the investigation of security incidents. But a number of issues present themselves. Firstly, how do we align the provider and customer definitions of the circumstances which will result in the disclosure of customer data? Details of the 'threshold for disclosure' may be outlined in the providers ToS or in their standard contract terms but will they provide sufficient detail to avoid disagreement about those terms. For example does '...*we will only disclose customer information to recognised law-enforcement agencies........*' require a simple request from law enforcement or an enforceable warrant. Secondly, effective utilisation of the cloning features of virtualization to preserve the chain of evidence for security investigations requires the use of trained *forensic experts* not typically part of the cloud contract. Unless the customer already has this capability in house this is a benefit which will probably never be realised.

- The cloud customer as *data controller*[53] may wish to utilise some of the common tools used by the security communities to ensure his information security stance (port scans, vulnerability assessment and penetration testing.) He may wish to adopt his own hardening procedures for servers that his data is stored on. The contractual terms of his contract may not allow this level of control but likewise contractual SLA may not commit the provider to ensuring these tools are utilised as part of the cloud security defences. How does the client ensure the effectiveness of the provider's security techniques in delivering a reasonable measure of security for his data? Again we have a possible governance gap.

---

[52] The term virtualization refers to the abstracting of the computer operating system from the hardware platform. The software that controls the abstraction is known as the hypervisor. By utilising this technology many small physical servers can be replaced by one large one running many instances of virtual machines. Examples of virtualization platforms include: Vmware, Xen, Microsoft virtual PC, Linux KVM and Virtual Box.

[53] Although we shall see in chapter 2 that for some cloud computing models the cloud provider must necessarily adopt some aspects of the data controller role and therefore accept some responsibility for the obligations levied by privacy and data protection legislation on the customer's data.

- Cloud services are provided on-demand.[54] The provider needs to accurately model the demand for his services and make sure sufficient investment in infrastructure is made. Inadequate *resource provisioning* will result in service unavailability and economic and reputation loss for both the provider and their customers. Whereas over provisioning of resource will lead to a lack of profitability for the provider.

- *Confidentiality* of customer data was touched on in our discussion of information ownership in section 1.2.4 above. A cloud architecture necessarily has, by virtue of design, more data in transit than traditional hosting architectures.[55] This data is considered 'in the cloud'. A traditional hosting model would normally employ VPN encryption technology but the cloud provider may be under no obligation to ensure ALL data flows are encrypted. This could present a vulnerability with opportunities for exploitation via snooping, 'man in the middle', spoofing or side channel attacks. An examination of how far a duty of confidentiality can create obligation on the provider to protect this information in the cloud will be provided in Chapter 2 'Information Security'.

- *Patentability* is also an ongoing issue. A lot of the Internet applications being designed and incorporated in the cloud use technology that is currently the subject of major law suits. Sun Microsystems created Java but find limited revenue streams emerging for themselves compared with more successful utilisation of the technology by rival companies. A case in point is the ongoing *Oracle v. Google* case involving Googles exploitation of this technology in their 'Android' product.

So cloud architectures are highly specialized in their design and customer resources are managed at different levels of abstraction within the cloud model. Each level of abstraction has its own set of vulnerabilities the mitigation of which will be the responsibility of the cloud provider or cloud customer depending on the model being implemented.[56] ENISA advises "*Cloud providers must set out a clear segregation of responsibilities that articulates the minimum actions customers must undertake*"[57] The provider must assume some responsibility for ensuring the customer knows what is expected of him in the relationship. In using a cloud service the customer necessarily gives control to the service provider for a number of issues which may be security related but retains

---

[54] See NIST definition at section 1.1 above.

[55] For example, data must be transferred in order to synchronise multiple distributed machine images, images distributed across multiple physical machines, between cloud infrastructure and remote web clients, etc.

[56] For a useful and informed breakdown of how these responsibilities vary over the different cloud computing architectures see ENISA – Cloud Computing, Benefits, risks and recommendations for information security. http://www.enisa.europa.eu/about-enisa page 66 'Division of responsibilities'

[57] ENISA – Cloud Computing, Benefits, risks and recommendations for information security. http://www.enisa.europa.eu/about-enisa

responsibility themselves for data security. The ENISA documentation also points out *"Customers must realize and assume their responsibility as failure to do so would place their data and resources at further risk"*. The division of responsibilities between provider and customer depends on the cloud model selected.[58] The ENISA documentation, in the absence of regulatory advice, is the nearest thing to a cloud computing best practice that the European Union produces. As a point of due diligence it would be prudent for both the provider and customer involved in negotiating a commercial cloud computing contract to take heed of the advice. To that end the technical aspects of a particular cloud model and the associated vulnerabilities and responsibilities for risk mitigation must be clearly understood at the outset. Technical as well as legal expertise needs to be engaged to avoid significant gaps in governance.

1.4 Trust, Cloud Governance and Standards

Trust is an amalgamation of a number of different attributes such as reliability, competence, security, truthfulness and honesty. The Oxford Reference Dictionary defines trust as "the firm belief in the reliability or truth or strength of an entity." A company engaged in the procurement of any type of information management system should perform an information security due diligence to assess the trust attributes and ensure the business and information security risks are well understood.

The Customer Perspective: Lack of control over the physical cloud infrastructure means that the role and content of SLA, contract and provider documentation is crucial for the customers own information risk management and due diligence. An adequate duty of care will involve pre-contract due diligence, adequate monitoring of transition states when moving to the cloud and development of adequate collaborative governance schemes. A customer considering cloud services will be hoping for sizable savings on IT costs and information processing. However part of that saving will need to be invested in adequate security screening of the provider including an ongoing audit strategy that will ensure the security standards are maintained. Further, collaborative governance structures should be developed and result in documented processes that feature in service level agreements and in contract terms.[59] To avoid the governance gaps already mentioned above the customer should make certain that security expertise both technical and legal is engaged during negotiation of SLA's to ensure their security requirements are contractually enforceable.

---

[58] IaaS, PaaS, SaaS or some of the hybrid deployments.
[59] CSA: Cloud Security Alliance, Security Guidance for Critical Areas of Focus in Cloud Computing V2.1 see page 31 'Governance recommendations'

The Provider Perspective: Although the law places ultimate responsibility for the security of personal and sensitive information with the data controller (UK DPA 1998) we have seen that argument does exist for some division of the controller role if not the controller responsibility to lie with the provider. The cloud customers due diligence and subsequent contract negotiation if prudently performed will try to put a contractual obligation for some of this responsibility onto the provider. The provider also needs to understand the dynamic here. Industry best practice as it matures will not consider an uninterested "that is not my problem" attitude to be a suitable approach to information security in the cloud. The law is unlikely to consider such an attitude a fair approach to contract formation. Instead a cloud provider should ensure adequate control over these aspects of its business by building **collaborative** governance structures and processes into its service delivery model.

While we wait for current cloud developments to bear fruit[60] we should look at how effective existing information and security standards[61] are in ensuring cloud security and building trust. This we will do fully in chapter 3 'Corporate Diligence and Compliance'

1.5 Chapter Summary

This chapter has introduced the concept of cloud computing and provided an overview of the issues pertaining to law, technology and governance in the cloud. The focus of the chapter has been on introducing the concept of reasonable security and relating this to information ownership and the division of responsibility and accountability for this information within the cloud environment. This discussion led to consideration of the governance gaps and begins to look at how these gaps can be plugged via contractual provision. All of these issues will be examined further in the coming chapters.

Chapter 2 will look deeper into Information Security and how data protection requirements can be maintained in the cloud.

---

[60] Standards currently in development that are being designed specifically with cloud computing in mind :
Open Security Architecture
Standardised security framework for cloud computing
A6 (Automated Audit, Assertion, Assessment, and Assurance API) working group
Trusted Cloud Initiative
Common Assurance Maturity Model (CAMM)
Federal Risk and Authorisation Management Program (FedRAMP)

[61] Current Standards are :
ISO 27001 (BS ISO/IEC 27001:2005, BS 7799-2:2005)
ISO 27002 (BS ISO/IEC 27002:2005, BS 7799-1:2005, BS ISO/IEC 17799:2005)
Control Framework for Information and related Technology (COBIT)
The Information Technology Infrastructure Library (ITIL)

Information Security

2.1   What is Information Security?

Data or information is at the heart of any 21st century modern organisation. The **confidentiality, integrity and availability** of this data must be protected in a comprehensive and systematic manner.[62] The Turnbull Report[63] has helped to place strategic responsibility for a company's information assets at the director level. Information security issues can now affect share price[64] making security a business issue. Poor information handling resulting in leaked information or public disclosure of sensitive information can affect a company's bottom line more than at anytime in the past.

The main legislation governing information handling in the UK is the Data Protection Act 1998. This act introduces the concepts of **data processor** and **data controller** which we must understand fully to clarify information security in the context of the cloud computing model.

Processing and Control

The most extensive control exerted by the legislation is on the 'data controller'. The directive states:

'controller' shall mean the natural or legal person, public authority, agency or any other body which alone or jointly with others determines the purposes and means of the processing of personal data; where the purposes and means of processing are determined by national or Community laws or regulations, the controller or the specific criteria for his nomination may be designated by national or Community law.[65]

---

[62] The principles of 'availability, integrity and confidentiality' are known as the AIC triad by (ISC)2 the security certification organisation offering the CISSP certification. All security controls and mechanisms are implemented to provide one or more of these principles. All threats and vulnerabilities are measured by their capability to compromise these principles.

[63] Turnbull Report: Internal Control: Guidance for directors on the Combined Code.

[64] The Turnbull approach is connected, through the Combined Code on Corporate Governance, to the Listing Rule disclosure requirements of the London Stock Exchange. Non-compliance with Turnbull would result in a disclosure on the annual report that could quickly attract adverse media comment and affect share price and credit rating.

[65] Directive 95/46/EC, Article 2(d)

The Data Protection Act subsequently states:

......(either alone or jointly or in common with other persons) determines the purposes for which and the manner in which personal data are, or are to be processed)[66]

How the roles of data processor and data controller are distributed in the cloud environment will have a bearing on where the obligations and possible liabilities for data breach lie. In SaaS and PaaS models the CSP can often determine the means of processing and thus fall under the definition of data controller. The ***Article 29 Data Protection working party*** has published a document designed to provide some guidance on the roles for complex environments.[67] Unfortunately for cloud computing the distinction can still remain unclear and each cloud service needs to be looked at on an individual basis to be clear on the demarcation points of responsibility.[68] This point should be discussed and feature in the contract term negotiations between the CSP and the customer.[69] It should be remembered that the ***7th data protection principle*** (DPA 1998, schedule 1) places the obligation for maintaining appropriate security measures firmly with the data controller and not the data processor. The controller is also responsible for selecting a processor who can provide satisfactory security guarantees.[70]

2.1.2 What Guarantee for Data Integrity

Many customers entering into cloud computing agreements may assume, from the nature of the service being supplied, that protection against: corruption, accidental deletion or security breach is implicit in the agreement. However a look at consumer orientated cloud computing offerings[71] shows an inherent tendency, in T&Cs, to disclaim liability for data integrity.

---

[66] Data Protection Act 1998 Section 1(1)

[67] Article 29 Data Protection Working Party: Opinion 1/2010 'on the concepts of controller and processor'

[68] This has been confirmed by the European Data Protection Supervisor, Peter Hustinx, in his speech *Data Protection and Cloud Computing under EU Law* on 13 April 2010, where he called for further guidance from the Working Party.

[69] Schedule 1, Pt 2, para 12 of the Act also obliges the formation of contract to control this relationship. Until legislation is available that clarifies the processor and controller aspects of the cloud computing model prudence would suggest both provider and client should make sure responsibilities are clearly outlined via contractual terms.

[70] DPA 1998, Schedule 1, Pt 2, para 11
[71] Such as those offered by Amazon, GoGrid and Microsoft.

" You bear sole responsibility for any and all data used in connection with the development, operation or maintenance of any software programs or services that use in connection with your access to or use of the services, including without limitation taking the steps necessary to back up such data, software programs or services." (Microsoft.Net)

The current position amongst providers is one where a guarantee of data integrity is a 'service add' incurring additional costs. This approach, prevalent amongst consumer orientated cloud providers, is becoming significant in shaping perceptions of the cloud. Clients looking for something more need to be aware of this tendency and insist on express terms on issues of responsibility for data integrity during the contract negotiation stage.

2.1.3   Tracking and Auditing Data in the Cloud

The 'on the move' nature of data can be a problem for customers who need to show auditable control. The ability to show where data has been accessed and 'processed' and control the nature of that processing is a fundamental component of an effective ***information security policy***. It seems obvious that a security model cannot provide reasonable security if the processes of law enforcement cannot be upheld. Law process requires evidence and effective audit trails are the beginnings of a 'chain of evidence'. Legal and regulatory systems in many countries create an obligation to assist forensic process. For instance in America ***Zubulake v. UBS Warburg LLC, 220 F.R.D. 212 (S.D.N.Y. 2003)*** clarifies the scope of a parties duty to preserve digital evidence during litigation and suggests punitive measures for deletion of such data. When negotiating a contract or assessing service level agreements customers should be aware that CSPs may back up data to many geographic locations and should seek assurance that the provider will be able to meet any litigation requirements as they arise.

2.2   Legal Data Disclosure

The first data protection principle is concerned with fair and lawful processing of data[72] but a significant exception exists for the purposes of law enforcement (s 29(1)). Further the circumstances in which providers will disclose customer data stored on the provider's cloud may have varying thresholds for disclosure.

All providers need to comply or actively contest court orders but the procedural safeguards in place vary from provider to provider dependent on their ethical stance on privacy issues.

---

[72] Data Protection Act 1998, Schedule 1

The social networking site facebook provides an example of one extremity of the available spectrum of approaches. Social networking sites and hosting sites are converging on their service offerings[73] so it is likely that the crafting of these sites to encourage behaviour not in keeping with conventional notions of privacy will play a part in lowering the expectation for certain cloud services.[74] EMI certainly think Michael Robertson has been crafty in crafting his new start up MP3tunes and selling it as an online storage facility where people can store their music files digitally and listen to them anywhere through a NET radio. The ongoing case (*EMI v. MP3tunes*) has privacy, security and even technology implications for the cloud computing model. During the court proceedings EMI demanded the handing over of all users music files stored in personal music lockers. The request was denied which appears to have been the correct decision since the request was rather like a fishing expedition. A more specific data request may prove more successful.[75]

Some CSPs disclose information in response to a request from law enforcement bodies (or even other Govnt agencies) rather than requiring an enforceable court order. Others may disclose information simply if it protects their own interests. Clarification of just when exactly data will be disclosed and the procedures involved should be sought at contract formation time by the parties involved. Standard form contracts modified from outsourcing agreements to cater for the cloud model are unlikely to have this level of detail.

2.3   Your Data and Contract Termination

Two issues present themselves when a cloud contract finishes.

1/ Can the customer gain access to data to retrieve for use elsewhere?

2/ Are there any assurances from the CSP on data deletion?

Cloud customers should ensure they are able to retrieve data from the CSP in a managed fashion which will provide satisfactory answers to the points above. A common term in contracts is to provide a grace period where the customer can access his data in order to effect

---

[73] Hosting sites such as Flickr now allow friends and family to upload photo's, blog and generally share information.

[74] See L Edwards and I Brown, "Data Control and Social Networking: irreconcilable Ideas?" in A Matwyshyn (ed) Harboring Data: Information Security, Law, and the corporation, Stanford Law Books, 2009 for good discussion on these issues.

[75] At present time a ruling may be 2-6 months away. The ruling should answer questions such as: Is cloud stored music legal? And do labels deserve more money when users store music via this cloud environment

migration or deletion of that data.[76] This would seem a reasonable approach but the customer should be aware of any exceptions which may provide for circumstances where the provider is under no obligation to preserve customer data. For example a termination clause in a contract may create different obligations on the provider for non-payment and termination for cause. Amazons T&C's note:

"Except as provided in Sections 3.7.1 and 3.7.2 above, we shall have no obligation to continue to store your data during any period of suspension or termination or to permit you to retrieve the same."[77]

This clause attempts to remove any obligation on the part of Amazon for preservation of customer data if the contract is terminated for reasons other than those expressly catered for. Other providers are even more extreme and state that data will be deleted immediately.[78]

Of course parties are free to contract on any terms they legally agree however terms such as those above could leave the service provider liable for criminal prosecution relating to the unauthorised deletion of customer data should a court at a later date decide the contract was ineffective or unfair in its formation or termination clauses. A better course to steer may be a hybrid approach where the provider is under no obligation to preserve data but neither will they delete the data and may even put in place a discretionary grace period.[79]

2.4 Security through Encryption

The main selling point for cloud computing is the efficiency with which the provider's global resources can be used to deliver services. As well as problems of jurisdiction the international nature of the data raises issues of security in transit. The technical problem is the same whether the communication is between the customer and the provider or entirely within the providers distributed datacentre. A provider should have encrypted links between its data centres ensuring meta-data in the cloud is carried over secure channels. Major cloud providers should ensure this is the case either within T&C's or service descriptions.[80] There is almost no point in

---

[76] For example see Amazon AWS's T&C's at http://aws.amazon.com/terms/.
[77] ibid
[78] See Apple's approach for its MobileMe product.

[79] This tends to be the approach followed by Microsoft in its cloud computing contracts. See T&C's for Microsoft.Net, Microsoft LiveMesh and Microsoft SQL Azure Database.

[80] The following appears on the web page of Dropbox *".......all transmission of file data and metadata occurs over an encrypted channel (SSL). Any data transferred from Dropbox over the Internet is securely encrypted and safe from interception and/or eavesdropping."* The appearance of this statement on a FAQ page relating to their

investing in expensive SAN (Storage Area Network) encryption technology for data storage if meta-data describing information about your data store is then transferred unencrypted over the Internet. A security system is only as good as its weakest link.

Encryption technology is expensive on cost and bandwidth utilisation. This may account for why some CSPs T&C's seem a little slack in their approach.[81] Legislation, although in general asking for security to be implemented via 'technical measures', does not specifically identify what those measures should be. This is illustrated in **Guin v. Brazos Education** where the courts found that the provisions of the **Gramm–Leach–Bliley Act (GLB)** although requiring an organisation to "*Develop, implement, and maintain a comprehensive written information security program*" and "*Design and implement information safeguards to control the risks you identify through risk assessment*", no requirement to include encryption is made.

Legislation such as UK **Regulation of Investigatory Powers Act 2000** and USA **Patriot Act 2001** allow a wide range of public servants access to data stored on computers in certain circumstances. Other jurisdictions will also have similar legislation in place. Although governments may have sufficient resource and processing power to break some forms of encryption it is unlikely that non-government organisations will have this capability. To keep your data relatively safe from prying eyes encryption seems to be a useful tool but there is a problem. This works great for cloud storage scenarios where data is simply encrypted, moved then stored in encrypted form. What if the cloud service is used for processing.[82] Data has to be unencrypted at the point of processing and if this is on a remote machine then this means data is unencrypted somewhere in the cloud. Some forms of data processing are then not legally permissable.[83]

Encrypting data may also limit the amount and depth of data monitoring which can be undertaken by the provider. All providers will monitor customer data to some degree if

---

service will arguably mean it is incorporated as an implied term into T&C's.

[81] 37Signals T&Cs state: "You understand that the technical processing and transmission of the Service, including your content, may be transferred unencrypted and involve (a) transmissions over various networks; and (b) changes to conform and adapt to technical requirements of connecting networks or devices." – http://basecamphq.com/terms

[82] Processing here means actual operations performed on the data. Legally speaking the data has already been processed by transferring the encrypted data and storing it in the cloud.

[83] For example personal medical data that is subject to the USA *Health Insurance Portability and Accountability Act 1996* — although some US citizens opt to share their own medical data via the cloud using the Google Health cloud service. (taken from **The Fog over the Grimpen Mire: Cloud Computing and the Law** *Miranda Mowbray)*

only to manage efficiency and quality of service (QoS) agreements. However encryption provides no security for some specific data flows related to frequency and volume of traffic and detailed analysis of these encrypted flows can reveal a surprising array of information.[84]

Some people believe service providers have a duty to monitor data uploads in certain circumstances in respect of copyright infringement. A limited amount of case law exists on this point but more can be expected in the future. The claim brought by Viacom against Google regarding uploads to YouTube was dismissed in June 2010 but the *Arista Records, LLC v. Usenet.com* case found against the service provider. Copyright issues are largely outside the scope of this document but these cases show the capacity for dispute.[85]

2.5   Chapter Summary

This chapter looked at what information security means in a cloud computing environment. It looked at the responsibilities levied on the data processor and data controller by the UK data protection act for the confidentiality, integrity and assurance of information. The relationship between reasonable security and law enforcement responsibilities for audit control and evidence gathering was discussed and the role of encryption as a technical measure was evaluated in a legal context. This chapter has allowed us to clarify what information security means in a cloud computing environment. The next chapter will look at how ineffective current standards frameworks are in upholding information security in the cloud and how contractual provision at the current time is essential in establishing reasonable security.

---

[84] See S Chen et al, "Side Channel Leaks in Web Applications: a Reality Today, a Challenge Tomorrow"(2010). http://reasearch.microsoft.com/apps/pubs/default.aspx?id=119060

[85] Viacom International and ors v YouTube and ors (23 June 2010) For decision and discussion http://static.googleusercontent.com/external_content/untrusted_dlcp/www.google.com/en//press/pdf/msj_decision .pdf

Chapter Three

Corporate Diligence and Compliance

"Security is both a feeling and a reality. And they are not the same"[86]

3.1   Trust, Diligence and Prudence

This chapter looks at how corporate diligence must adequately evaluate the security, legal and compliance issues affecting the level of trust a cloud customer can reasonably vest in a CSP. Corporate diligence is responsible for ensuring critical business decisions are based on reasonably assessed levels of trust. Trust ill-placed may, in the extreme, be considered negligent.

The CSA (http://www.cloudsecurityalliance.org) is a non-profit organisation currently developing a best practice framework designed to create a measured security assurance for cloud computing architectures. The diagram below outlines how security and compliance can be mapped to the cloud model in a manner which helps identify gaps in an organisations compliance model. This model is useful in helping organisations place security controls appropriately especially now when widespread lack of understanding about the security gaps in the cloud compliance model is creating risk and potential liability for both customer and provider.

---

[86] Essay on "The Psychology of Security" by Bruce Schneir (2008) - www.schneier.com/essay-155.html

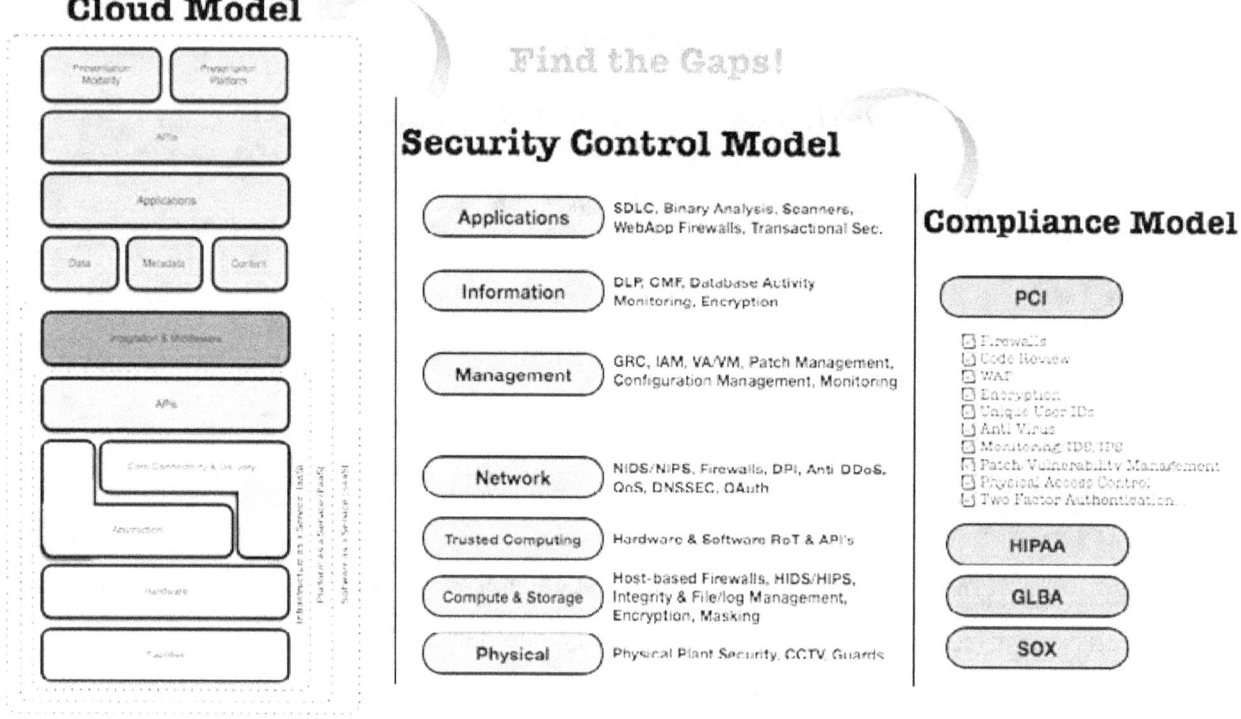

Fig 3.1 Mapping the cloud model to the security and compliance model (CSA, 2009)

3.2 Understanding the Division of Liability

Liability can arise through essentially three aspects of a cloud service:[87] lawfulness of content, security incidents and European or other data protection law status.

With regards to *lawfulness of content* the cloud customer will always have full liability but the provider may carry an intermediary liability which he may not be aware of.[88] Article 2 of EU Directive 98/48/EC [89] calls for, with regards to any information society services, *"Administrative cooperation in accordance with Article 7a of the Treaty"* between customers and providers. [90] Article 2 of EU Directive 2000/31/EC[91] in (b) defines the 'service provider' and in Article 12 and 15 provides exceptions for this role designed to deal with the conduit

---

[87] ENISA, 'Cloud Computing, Benefits, Risks and Recommendations for Information Security. Page 66.
[88] See the case **Cartoon Network v. CSC Holdings** for a useful discussion on primary and intermediary liabilities in relation to an Internet service provision (in this case video content).
[89] Amending Directive 98/34/EC laying down a procedure for the provision of information in the field of technical standards and regulations.
[90] Para 14 referring to the treaty establishing the European Community.
[91] On certain legal aspects of information society services, in particular electronic commerce, in the internal market.

nature of some traffic profiles.[92] Although these exceptions do protect the CSP from most content related liabilities for traffic merely passing through its sphere of influence Article 12 (3) states:

"3. This Article shall not affect the possibility for a court or administrative authority, in accordance with Member States' legal systems, of requiring the service provider to terminate or prevent an infringement."

Although there is no general requirement to monitor traffic on its infrastructure an obligation is placed on a provider to act when made aware of unlawful behaviour. Depending on the nature of the inaction this can also expose the provider to other areas of law such as defamation and libel. In the UK the case of ***Laurence Godfrey v. Demon Internet Limited, (1999)*** Demon failed to act when notified by the plaintiff, of a defamatory email on an Internet Usenet discussion group. Although the plaintiff had asked for the forged email to be removed Demon chose to ignore the request and allow it to remain until it naturally expired. The decision, in favour of the plaintiff centred round the fact the defendant "chose to store" rather than remove the email. More recent case law expands and clarifies this view. The case of ***Viacom International and ors v YouTube and ors*** (23 June 2010, unreported) although relating to copyright infringement deals with a service providers obligation (or lack thereof) to monitor customer data. The US court (New York) granted summary judgment to Google (who now own YouTube) holding that they could use the safe harbor provisions of DMCA. Although they had knowledge of general infringement the notice period had not been sufficient for them to act effectively on it.

The protection offered to CSPs in the US by the DMCA safe harbor provisions has been further addressed in ***Perfect 10 Inc. v. CCBill LLC***[93] and ***UMG Recordings, Inc. v. Veoh Networks Inc.***[94] In Perfect 10 the service providers responsibility to block repeat offenders is emphasised and UMG deals with protection for service providers that simply reformat third-party data.[95]

The 'administrative cooperation' referred to above suggests an obligation on effective communication between customer and CSP for all aspects of a cloud service (an information society service). Creation of effective governance frameworks for administration of these services would seem to be an implied requirement of the directive and subsequent

---

[92] Article 12 "mere conduit" and Article 15 "no general obligation to monitor"

[93] Perfect 10 Inc. v. CCBill LLC, 488 F.3d 1102 (9th Cir. 2007)

[94] UMG Recordings, Inc. v. Veoh Networks, Inc., 2008 WL 5423841 (C.D. Cal. 2008)

[95] See also Io Group v. Veoh Networks, Inc. This case illuminates DMCA safe harbor protections for third party content.

regulations.[96] Prudent contract negotiation should certainly take this view. As courts and the legal system become more aware of the workings of cloud computing and the governance gaps which can result from poor or uninformed planning, a service provider who leaves critical aspects of service governance (such as security) up to the customer may be looked on as exerting unfair influence on the contract as a result of a 'selective amnesia' when dealing with these issues. The concept of 'fitness for purpose' has been developing in commercial law for quite some time. In *St Albans City and District Council v International Computers Ltd [1996] 4 All ER 481* the Judge in his remarks commented on this shift from caveat emptor to caveat venditor and the trend continues in the later cases *Peglar v Wang (UK) Limited 2000* and *Beta Computers (Europe) Ltd v Adobe Systems (Europe) Ltd* which we look at in section 3.4 below.

With respect to *security incidents* the roles and responsibilities for customer and provider need to be carefully defined. These demarcation points will vary greatly depending on the particular cloud model being implemented (PaaS, IaaS or SaaS). American court cases such as *Columbia Pictures, Inc. v. Bunnell* and *Tomlinson v. El Paso Corporation* suggest that when a cloud customer has some control over the technical aspects of data handling in the cloud the courts will expect that customer to adhere to judicial process and hand over documentation and data when required (e-discovery requirements for example). This will have a bearing for IaaS customers where that control is very much an element of the 'self provisioned' part of the service. For standard term contracts the customer must be sure he understands what he is responsible for. Within negotiated contracts the customer and provider should clearly define their responsibilities. A useful list of how these responsibilities divide for the three cloud models is provided by ENISA.[97]

In order to deliver the benefits of cloud computing to its customers providers offer low cost commodity services rather than tailor made services. Some aspects of any service will therefore be of a one size fits all nature which introduces additional risk. Standard contract clauses should be reviewed in light of the cloud model. Specifically the clauses limiting liability should be carefully assessed according to the divisions of liability as seen through detailed analysis of the service offering. Attention should be focused on where obligation falls for notifications such as: data protection, law enforcement, data transfer, security breach and intellectual property matters (derivative works for example).

---

[96] The Electronic Commerce (EC Directive) Regulations 2002 (SI 2002 No. 2013)
[97] see note 80

3.2.1 Liability in the Supply Chain

In some instances a CSP will subcontract aspects of the security of a cloud service to a third party. This can include operations such as: external user authentication services, Intrusion detection, forensic services or even the maintenance and operation of the underlying cloud infrastructure itself. It may even involve the use of third parties by third parties! (nth parties). Proper governance should recursively look at all providers involved in the service delivery. A company's *Information Assurance* department (both customer and provider) should be tasked with the creation of questionnaire's which clarify the pertinent issues of service responsibility. The questions asked will vary greatly but should cover the following aspects of the service:

- Define the outsourced services present in the supply chain that are key to security.

- Detail the procedures used to control third party access to your infrastructure.

- Is the SLA provision offered by third parties in line with the SLA agreement you offer your customers?

- How do you maintain third party SLA levels?

- Are controls determined by a security policy applied to the third party via contractual clauses?[98]

Effective use of these questionnaires can ensure the liability landscape is understood and responsibility falls where intended. Should an organisation end up in a legal dispute they provide evidence of a prudent approach to managing the governance gaps currently inherent in the cloud computing model.

3.3 Building Trust through Adherence to Standards.

Industry standards serve to create predictability within implementation paradigms.[99] Predictability in turn enables trust. The lack of cloud-specific standards is not, at this early stage,

---

[98] For help with creating the level of granularity which will produce effective questionnaires see ENISA, 'Cloud Computing, Benefits, risks and recommendations for information security' page 71 (Information Assurance Requirements). Also see Appendix 1 for comprehensive list of questions utilised during research phase of this report.
[99] Executives Guide to Cloud Computing: Eric A. Marks, Bob Lozano

a barrier to the adoption of cloud computing. The financial benefit available through cost saving on infrastructure costs is fuelling development. However as the model develops maturity the bigger picture will become more relevant. Disgruntled customers will seek to change their CSP. It is common standards that generally facilitate interchangeability helping to reduce risk for customers and thus driving further investment in the industry. The development of formal widely accepted cloud standards is therefore essential but for the moment the de-facto security standards and best practice developed for the conventional computing industry will have to do. Here we look at the current security standards available and assess their relevance to cloud computing.

ISO 27001 /27002 (BS ISO/IEC 27001/27002:2005). This standard is widely used by industry to assess the security posture of businesses. The certification scheme used is widely regarded to say that an organisation has implemented sound security practice and business process is carried out in a controlled manner. Unfortunately the certification scheme may not be very relevant, as it stands at present, to cloud computing. This is because of the generic rather than specific nature of cloud services. One customer's services may be implemented and governed slightly differently than another's especially on IaaS and PaaS deliveries. Although the gleaning of practical benefits from the certification scheme may require some work, achievement of the standard does show a willingness to engage in security best practice.

To achieve the practical benefits of the ISO27001/2 standard[100] vendor and customer will need to work together on development of the ISMS.[101] Scaling this for multiple cloud customers could mean substantial security administration overhead and a re-working of the organisations standard compliance regime.

Control Framework for Information and related Technology (COBIT).[102] The cloud computing model may not be suitable for all types of data. One of the first tasks to be undertaken, probably by the Information Assurance dept, is assessing the adequacy of the solution against the organisations business model. The COBIT framework will help in defining

---

[100] Procedure and document control, internal assurance through audit, controlled risk assessment methodology, risk mitigation plans, effective security reporting etc.

[101] The Information Security Management System (ISMS) is a four phase management structure (plan, do, check and act) at the core of the ISO standard.

[102] "framework for IT governance and control , it supports toolset that allows managers to bridge the gap between control requirements, technical issues and business risks" (ISACA, 2010).

the IT strategy[103] for cloud computing and in assuring that the governance framework will be able to manage responsibility and accountability for the governance gaps which appear from adoption of a cloud computing model.[104] The COBIT 'maturity model' will help assess the effectiveness and relevance of any new governance processes created.

One of the biggest problems with cloud computing is the potential customer's lack of visibility of the cloud security footprint. Standards help create a framework that everyone can understand and so build trust. Frameworks in development at present include: A6, Trusted cloud initiative, Common Assurance Maturity Model (CAMM) and Federal Risk and Authorisation Management Program (FedRAMP). These will bear fruit in the future but provide very little help at present. The ISO27000 and COBIT standards mentioned above although pre-dating the cloud computing era are mature, tried and tested standards. The 'Cloud Computing Pattern' developed by the **Open Security Architecture**[105] is a more recent development which provides a mapping to the ISO and COBIT standards. It provides a useful reference for those CSPs looking to foster client trust through leveraging the ISO security and COBIT governance frameworks.

3.3.1 Security Standards, Certification and the Contract

Contracts are typically negotiated and constructed by business managers and lawyers who have only a vague idea of the technology involved. They will rely on IT staff or consultancy services to clarify technical areas but the requirements are ultimately determined by the lawyers. When conducting due diligence prior to entering into a contract with a CSP the customer should be proportionate with its demands for certification standards.[106] Focusing on the sensitivity of the data involved will help customers achieve a balanced and financially viable solution. Not all data will require SAS 70 type II or ISO27002 protection which tends to be expensive. However other data security requirements may be linked to legal compliance such as HIPAA or PCI-DSS. Where this is the case the customer should draw attention to these in the contract and get assurances from the CSP that it has the experience and commitment to

---

[103] COBIT process P01:- "Define a strategic IT plan."
[104] Especially useful will be COBIT Process DS2:- "Manage third-party services"
[105] SP-011, Cloud Computing Pattern – Open Security Architecture.
http://www.opensecurityarchitecture.org/cms/library/patternlandscape/251-pattern-cloud-computing
[106] The standards themselves suggest this proportionality. Almost all security standards involve a risk based approach to the assessment of threats and vulnerabilities.

meet this compliance requirement.

If a vendor asserts that they use a particular governance or security framework this shows awareness of the issues but doesn't really say anything about the control measures it has chosen to adopt. For instance the CoBit[107] framework is used regularly by companies but this says nothing about how customer data is to be secured and as such is not a useful contractual reference. Security standards such as FIPS 200[108] and SP-800-53[109] in the USA and ISO27001[110] internationally can be more useful in contracts for providing a high level of security assurance to customers.

Cloud contracts involving payment card data are another area where specific industry standards are called for. The PCI-DSS standard is not a law but a contractual obligation which will be enforced, by the payment card companies themselves, with fines and penalties for non-compliance.[111] Any cloud contract involving the handling of such data processing activities should specifically reference the standard and the customer should include all activities which will be expected from the vendor (CSP) in achieving and maintaining compliance.[112]

3.4 Compliance and Audit

As cloud computing develops as a means of 'outsourcing' key business activities the customer must make sure he maintains compliance with his security policy and legislative and regulatory requirements. Auditors and assessors may not fully understand the cloud

---

[107] Control Objectives for Information and Related Technology, a standard framework for IT governance and information management controls published by the IT Governance Institute and the Information Systems Audit and Control Association (ISACA).

[108] "Minimum Security Requirements for Federal Information and Information Systems" – FIPS 200
[109] SP 800-53, NIST Special Publication "Recommended Security Controls for Federal Information Systems".

[110] In circumstances where the customer requires greater assurance through third-party verification of security measures, the customer should consider requiring a certification of compliance with ISO 27001, which states management control requirements for information security management systems. ISO 27001 requires management to systematically assess the organization's security risks and impacts, design and implement security controls to address unacceptable risks, and adopt management procedures to review and revise those controls over time. When an organization self-certifies compliance with ISO 27001, or obtains certification from a third party, it normally refers as well to ISO 27002, because that provides implementation guidance for the selected controls. (*Taken from* Information Security Standards and Certifications in Contracting).

[111] See http://www.itgovernance.co.uk/pci_dss.aspx for a good breakdown of just what it is and what is involved in becoming compliant.
[112] For example completion of self-assessment questionnaire or requiring a compliance assessment by a Qualified Security Assessor.

perspective and the customer must be prepared to argue his case. To that end the cloud customer should understand:

- The applicability of the cloud model for any regulated service requirements.

- The division of the compliance responsibilities between provider and customer.

- The provider's ability to show evidence of compliance requirements. Especially important when the provider is showing compliance on behalf of the customer.

- Any gaps in understanding of the cloud service between the provider and the auditor.

Compliance and audit obligations should be addressed in contract. Customers will need the ability to audit the provider. This should, where possible, be met in a 'Right to Audit Clause' especially where the provider is handling the customer's regulatory compliance responsibilities.

Several compliance regulations specifically require a risk based approach to utilisation of third parties for elements of the service provision.[113] Customers will need to vet provider processes used to engage third parties who act on behalf of the provider or again have contractual clauses which create an obligation on the provider to meet all compliance requirements. Customers should create processes to collect and store evidence which shows the provider is meeting their compliance requirements. This should include audit logs, activity reports, system configuration change reports, change management histories etc. Much of this information may itself come from the CSP.

As already outlined in Chapter 1 a lot of cloud providers will want to contract on their standard terms. These terms will in many cases contain clauses attempting to limit liability for certain behaviour which creates governance gaps affecting the customer. Some recent case law relating to the effectiveness (or not) of certain exclusions or limitations of liability will have some relevance here. The case *Peglar v Wang (UK) Limited 2000* shows that for a party to ensure its exclusion clauses are effective they need to make sure those clauses are not held to be within the provisions of the UK's Unfair Contract Terms Act (UCTA). Although before the rise of cloud

---

[113] PCI DSS requirement 12.8 for example requires documented policies and procedures for interfacing with third party providers.

computing this case did involve the provision of IT services including infrastructure and software.

The Wang ruling has relevance for our pursuit of 'reasonableness' when applied to security provisions in the cloud computing world. Section 11(5) UCTA introduces a test for 'reasonableness' of contractual terms and we have already discussed how governance gaps can be 'plugged' by contractual obligation levied on the cloud provider. The providers approach to exclusion of liability (tempered by the foil provided by the UCTA's reasonableness test) may need to pay heed to prudent risk assessment in order to avoid damages such as those incurred by Wang. Wang relied on two exemption clauses fairly typical of those found in cloud contracts. The first excluded liability for *"loss of anticipated profits or of data"* and the second barred actions more than 2 years after the causal event. A fundamental of the law of liability is that one claiming an exclusion of liability has to show that he comes within it.[114] The Judge in his decision found it was unreasonable in view of their own misrepresentations for Wang to rely on exclusion clauses limiting their liability for breach of contract.

A more recent case adds another 'cloud dimension' to the mix involving the provision of software services and expertise. The case ***Kingsway Hall Hotel Ltd v Red Sky IT (Hounslow) Ltd [2010] EWHC 965 (TCC) HHJ*** examines the use and enforceability of exclusion clauses in a contract for the provision of software and related services. In this case Kingsway relied on Red Sky's advice on the service provision and accepted their standard term contract.[115] On becoming dissatisfied with the service provided by Red Sky, Kingsway sought compensation through the courts. This case provides some guidance on how the provisions of the Unfair Contract Terms Act 1977 will be applied to software service contracts and shows that suppliers need to conduct themselves according to the 'reasonableness test' if they do not wish to undermine or make invalid fundamental contractual protections. A CSP who chooses to ignore the governance gaps resulting from the uptake of their cloud service or sees this simply as the customer's problem could find themselves suffering the same fate as Wang.

3.5 Chapter Summary

Security responsibility in many cases is facilitated through the use of standards but it is not sufficient to simply ask for a particular certification to be in evidence. It is important to assess the

---

[114] *The Glendarroch* [1894] P 226, 231, per Lord Esher.
[115] http://www.legal500.com/books/l500/developments/11006

type of data involved and to clearly address how specific security measures will be implemented and controlled by the provider or the customer to address the gaps which arise almost inevitably through the adoption of a cloud computing service model. Express reference to any controlling standards (such as PCI) or laws should be made where possible and contractual audit rights should be included to ensure customers are able to verify for themselves that their compliance needs are being met by the provider. In light of the well documented governance gaps both customer and cloud provider need to be clear on the division of security responsibilities. Liability can be created for either through a failure to address these divisions. Contractual provision seems a reasonable approach to addressing the issues but the effectiveness of contractual clauses to limit liability are tempered with the reasonableness test of the UCTA. Creation of effective contract requires prudent discussion and negotiation between the parties involving relevant technical expertise as well as the legal and regulatory requirements.

Chapter Four

Putting it all together

4.1 The Pursuit of Reasonableness

Cloud computing relies on the Internet. The Internet is inherently insecure, unmanaged and anyone on it is vulnerable to attack from anyone else. Already major cloud computing providers have suffered significant service outages[116] some as a result of malicious hacker activity. Indeed at a recent DEF CON[117] conference 89% of hackers and IT security experts polled indicated that weaknesses in cloud computing services would be the latest vulnerabilities to be targeted by the hacking community.[118]

We have seen that many of the benefits of cloud computing are accompanied by risks arising from changes and omissions within corporate governance. Ambiguities arising through jurisdictional issues about data location create privacy concerns that need to be addressed. US regulatory frameworks and EU privacy legislation will inevitably influence cloud service provider behaviour. Under EU law there must be a legal basis for processing personal data.[119] In a cloud context a business will rely on the freely given consent of data subjects or on contract fulfilment to create this basis. We have seen that EU law requires data controllers to implement appropriate "technical and operational measures"[120] to provide reasonable and adequate security control for that personal data. These operational measures must include notification schemes on data breach.[121] Cloud customers because of the increased level of public access to the cloud should insist on data breach notifications from the provider via their contractual terms.

Providing guidance to companies interested in adopting a cloud computing solution is a difficult matter due to the rapidly evolving legal landscape. Legal and Regulatory bodies around the

---

[116] Amazon aws outage:
http://www.datacenterknowledge.com/archives/2009/07/19/outage-for-amazon-web-services/ .
Amazon EC2 outage: http://news.cnet.com/8301-1009_3-10413951-83.html
Microsoft BPOS outage: http://www.networkworld.com/news/2010/091310-microsoft-cloud-outage.html
Google Apps outage: http://www.fredberinger.com/google-outage-a-broken-cloud

[117] DEFCON is the world's longest running and largest underground hacking conference. www.defcon.org
[118] OUT-LAW News article 'Hackers say they are targeting cloud computing.'
[119] Charter of Fundamental Rights Article 8(2), or Regulation (EC) 45/2001- OJ L8 of 12.01.200
[120] DPA 1998, 7th Data Protection Principle.
[121] See note 50

world are trying to deal with the privacy and data security implications of the cloud computing model but progress is slow.[122] As well as the legal concerns a whole host of non legal problems such as: cloud migration strategies and service gaps resulting from Internet service outage need to taken into consideration by a company before deciding to move to the cloud.

In this chapter we shall look at strategies for effectively handling the data protection and information security obligations introduced by cloud computing in such a manner as to warrant the tag of 'reasonable' in a legal context. We will also look at some possible future developments with regards to management of security policy and regulatory control.

4.2   Dealing with Data Protection

A cloud computing service can be: email services, messaging services, virtual desktops, project management, HR, sales management, application development, health services, and billing. If the take-up of cloud computing is to reach anything near the heights being proposed for it *personal data (including sensitive data) will be processed*.

The Data Protection Directive[123] will apply if the 'data controller' is established in the EU or if he uses equipment for processing of sensitive information which itself resides in the EU.[124] Our examination so far of vendor, customer relationships in the cloud has placed the customer in the role of data controller and the CSP, in varying degrees, as an external processor.[125] The customer must be clear on his responsibility when collecting and processing information (which should be done in accordance with sections 7 and 10 of the directive) but should look to manage contractually the data protection relationship with the CSP.[126] The cloud customer should look for the inclusion of a specific data protection clause in negotiations. Specifically the clause should work to ensure the following:

- The CSP will cooperate with the data controller (customer) in ensuring the data subjects rights under sections 1 and 2 of the Directive are upheld.[127]

---

[122] See note 90

[123] DIRECTIVE 95/46/EC

[124] See Section 4 of Directive 95/46/EC

[125] External because the provider is not part of the controllers company.

[126] This is not always possible. A lot of small to medium sized businesses will be faced with a 'take it or leave it' market place where the only option for negotiation is the choice of cloud vendor. We are primarily concerned here with the larger customer who is able to negotiate his service provision.

[127] Section 1, contains Article 6 relating to fair and lawful processing. Section 2, contains Article 7 relating to consent and necessity.

- Article 17 of the directive requires the controller to "implement appropriate technical and organizational measures." A great deal of this requirement whether IaaS, PaaS or SaaS will need to be implimented by the provider. The customer (controller) should maintain this by placing a requirement on the provider for information security breach notification and an undertaking for swift problem resolution.

- Data transfers to countries outwith the EU which do not meet the levels of protection outlined in Article 25(2)[128] and are not protected by a Safe Harbor agreement will require data subject consent or should be subject to contractual control. This is a messy area of law at present and the cloud customer should reflect ernestly on whether the cloud service meets his needs. Creating effective contractual clauses to deal with data transfer within global virtual datacentres may prove unworkable. Some CSP's are now offering geographically zoned cloud services to address some of these issues (see below). If subject consent is not a practical consideration the zoned approach may be the way forward.

A complication is that although personal and sensitive data can circulate freely within the EEA, laws are not consistent across all countries. ENISA has suggested that a certification standard for a minimum level of data protection across member states would be useful.[129]

4.2.1 Negotiating the Data Protection Clause

CLOUD PROVIDER	CUSTOMER
A) Large company – **strong ability to negotiate contract clauses**	SME – **Weak or lacking ability to negotiate contract clauses**
B) Both the customer and the provider have the **ability to negotiate contract clauses**	
C) SME – **Weak ability to negotiate contract clauses**	Large company or public administration - **may negotiate contract clauses**

Table 1: Three Cloud Corporate Scenarios[130]

---

[128] "The adequacy of the level of protection afforded by a third country shall be assessed in the light of all the circumstances surrounding a data transfer operation or set of data transfer operations; particular consideration shall be given to the nature of the data, the purpose and duration of the proposed processing operation or operations, the country of origin and country of final destination, the rules of law, both general and sectoral, in force in the third country in question and the professional rules and security measures which are complied with in that country." Article 25(2)

[129] ENISA – Cloud Computing - Benefits, Risks and Recommendations for Information Security. Annex 1
[130] *ibid*

Not all corporate relationships have the same capacity for contract negotiation. Most relationships will follow scenarios A and B outlined in the table above. Many cloud computing services currently mentioned in the press are offered via fixed T&Cs and SLA agreements that are non negotiable (A in the table). A cloud customer who decides to utilise cloud computing in this way will need to determine whether any data protection clauses present are adequate to guarantee the customers compliance requirements. A cursory glance at most of the CSP T&Cs already discussed[131] show that most of these non negotiable cloud offerings are unsuitable for data handling which involves sensitive information and the use of these services for the processing of such could be deemed as misinformed at least (negligent at worst!?)

When there is a capacity to negotiate (scenarios B and C in table 1), the requirement for 'appropriate technical measures' should feature in the data protection discussions. Any reference to security standards and requirements[132] should be made in a formal SLA agreement as part of the contract. Reports generated by the service provider can in turn be used by the customer to meet the compliance requirements. The contract should also cover any remedies which result should a data breach occur and for substantial data breaches this may even feature as an instance which can lead to unilateral termination of the contract.

4.3   Dealing with Confidentiality

As well as processing sensitive information relating to individuals the cloud service may handle information which is of a confidential nature. This is any information which if disclosed would have an adverse affect on the customers business. This information can be processed in two different ways.

1. Data can be operated on within the cloud to produce new data sets. The data changes.

2. Data can be transferred and stored within the cloud but remains unchanged.

Encryption is commonly used to provide confidentiality and integrity. For processing as described by '2' above it is ideal. However where computational operations are required on data

---

[131] See notes 69 to 72

[132] This could involve regular reports generated by the provider from Intrusion Detection Systems (IDS) or Security Event Management (SEM) systems.

it will first need to be decrypted. The act of decryption in the cloud significantly changes the security footprint. Cloud customers must fully understand how their service will be delivered, details of data storage methods and whether the data will be 'clear text' at any point within the cloud. Customers should seek to deal with these issues contractually using 'confidentiality clauses' or 'non disclosure agreements' which outline in detail how their 'know how'[133] and secret information will be protected. Specifically they should clarify whether their data will appear unencrypted at any point. Use of a confidentiality clause will create certainty and a contractual obligation on the provider through the establishment of a confidential relationship.

Customers may also be concerned about the knowledge that the CSP will gain from access to their data through provisioning of the service. Both the law of confidentiality and copyright have something to say about information gleaned from information. *Feist v. Rural* is an important case in copyright law establishing that information on its own is not enough to provide it with copyright protection. Further attempts at protecting collections of data in the US have largely failed.[134] However, **Seager Limited v Copydex Limited [1967] 2 All ER 415** may bring some piece of mind for the cloud customer. In this case Lord Denning MR ruled that under equity law a person or organisation that receives information in confidence cannot take unfair advantage of it and must seek the consent of the person who gave it. This is also true even if no confidentiality clause is in place. In **Craigslist, Inc. v. Naturemarket, Inc** Craigslist won a $1.3 million judgement against a software provider who 'scraped' email addresses and other information as background tasks whilst posting listings to the Craigslist web page. This has some relevance for service provider behaviour, especially for data mining activities undertaken by the provider on customer data. Although it doesn't in itself prevent such activities it may require the provider to make these activities clear to the customer and seek his consent through contractual negotiation. If a confidentiality clause is present it should clarify this through the giving or not of consent.

4.3.2 Negotiating the Confidentiality Clause

Customers should seek contractual agreement on the points raised above (4.3). As with data protection a specific clause should be sought that will define the division of responsibility and liability for data confidentiality. Specific technical measures such as use of encryption should be appended in a technical annex to the confidentiality agreement. The customer should also

---

[133] 'Know how' is defined within *Commission Regulation (EC) No 772/2004 of 27 April 2004*
[134] Ekstrand, Victoria S. (2002). "Drawing Swords After *Feist*: Efforts to Legislate the Database Pirate". *Communication Law and Policy* 7 (3): 317–341. doi:10.1207/S15326926CLP0703_04.

evaluate the potential damage a confidentiality breach will have on his business and create a provision within the agreement which will reflect the damage he may sustain. Substantial breaches should lead to reparation costs and the ability to unilaterally terminate the contract.

A confidentiality agreement is only of use so long as the information being considered remains secret or private. The infamous case of **Attorney-General v Guardian Newspapers Ltd [1990] 1 AC 109** involving Peter Wright and the Spy Catcher novel illustrates the point. Lord Keith of Kinkel, Lord Brightman, Lord Griffiths, Lord Goff of Chieveley and Lord Jauncey of Tullichettle upheld the Attorney General's appeal finding the Sunday Times Newspaper in breach of a duty confidence.The newspaper in publishing extracts of the book two days early had no defence of 'prior publication.' The case clarifies the relationship of confidential information to third party knowledge. A duty of confidentiality precludes disclosure and any third parties aware of the confidential nature of information are bound by a similar duty unless outweighed by public interest. This serves to strengthen the obligation on the cloud provider to protect the customers confidential information but also outlines the customers responsibility to clarify the expectation levied on the provider.

4.4   Dealing with Professional Negligence

The type of services that a customer may entrust to a cloud provider can include: payroll services, email, virtual desktops, project planning and other internal functions. A failure in any of these 'outsourced' services may result in a cloud customer being exposed to a tortuous liability resulting in actions for damages. A duty of care can be established by statute[135] but developing common law shows that a duty of care can also be inherent in the service provision. In *Bell v. Michigan Council*, for example, the court held that the *"defendant did owe plaintiffs a duty to protect them from identity theft by providing some safeguards to ensure the security of their most essential confidential identifying information."*

On the other hand it is perfectly possible through abusive use of the cloud service that damage could result for the CSP. Service Level Agreements (SLAs) and "Liability" and "Indemnity" clauses should be used to clearly define the general duties and responsibilities as well as the

---

[135] For instance in *Guin v. Brazos Education* the court acknowledges that a duty of care is established by the Gramm-Leach-Bliley Act (although unfortunately for the plaintiff in this case he was unable to make use of it).

division of liabilities.

Given the importance that the choice of CSP has for the cloud customer's business, and given that careful selection of provider is likely to have been based on reputation, professionalism and technical abilities customers may subsequently be reluctant to see the CSP subcontracting part of the service delivery to a third party. The customer in such circumstances should look for written guarantees and warranties from the CSP on the 'fit for purpose' status of these contracts. Changes in that status should require prompt notification and an option to terminate the contract if unsatisfied with the details of the providers new service provision.[136] In order to facilitate a smooth transition from one provider to another the customer should look to include contractual provisions that include procedures to migrate without imposing technical or substantial financial cost.[137]

4.5   Don't Panic! Stay CAMM

We have shown that within the cloud computing environment the governance relationships between the customer, CSP and other third parties are key to maintaining control over exposure to liability. Governance gaps easily arise within these relationships when an organisation decides to move some of its service functions into the cloud. Corporate Information Assurance departments are currently struggling to plug these gaps however one of the most promising developments has been the beginnings of the '*Common Assurance Maturity Model*' (CAMM).[138] The CAMM 'mission statement' is shown below.

---

[136] See ENISA 2009 and Council of Europe 2010 Cloud Computing and Its Implications on Data Protection

[137] "It is extremely important to avoid 'vendor lock-in' in order to prevent barriers to market entry, fully benefit from increasing variety of cloud services and models, and foster competition in this emerging market. Contracts that do not contemplate procedures to migrate from the selected CSP to another and/or impose restrictions on this matter should be avoided."-- **Paolo Balboni** – ICT Lawyer: www.paolobalboni.eu. Steering Committee Member of the Common Assurance Maturity Model (CAMM). Selected Legal Consultant for the European Networks and Information Security Agency (ENISA) studies: *Cloud Computing Risk Assessment* and *Security and Resilience in Gov Clouds*

[138] http://common-assurance.com/

> <u>Mission Statement</u>
>
> Provide an ***objective, consistant and complete*** trust *framework* to ***transparently*** assure ***information risk management maturity*** across the ***supply chain.***[139]

This is an extension of the conclusions we arrived at in section 3.3 above where we noted that service providers should try to create customer trust through the pursuit of security industry standards managed through the CoBit framework. The CAMM approach develops this idea within a framework specifically designed for cloud computing and sizable third party 'outsourcing'.

Current information assurance strategies are designed for self contained IT architectures. However, cloud computing is delivering IT services through supply chains that could involve many component organizations that have varying degrees of transparency and control. The CAMM framework aims to create a common trust framework which brings audit efficiencies and allows security comparisons to be made about cloud vendors and other third party services. CAMM utilises security standards such as ISO27000 and PCI-DSS as well as elements of the CoBit framework. Organisations will be able to leverage existing investment in these standards towards utilising the CAMM framework. The framework will allow informed risk decisions to be made based on comparative assurance levels for different service implementations. Effectiveness will be dependent on a collaborative approach between the key industry organizations, regulators and standardization bodies. For full details on the CAMM workings see their vision doc.[140]

4.6   Towards Cloud Interoperability

The single most important issue which needs to be addressed if cloud computing is to realise the heights predicted for it is the creation of a cloud standard framework which will

---

[139] CAMM vision document:
http://common-assurance.com/wp-content/uploads/Common-Assurance-Maturity-Model-vision.pdf
[140] Ibid

maintain data security and integrity while promoting vendor interoperability.[141] Several organizations are already working on this: Cloud Computing Interoperability Forum (CCIF), Open Grid Forum's new Open Cloud Computing Interface Working Group and the DMTF incubator[142] amongst others. Cloud interoperability means different things to different people and although there is a lot of activity on this front there is a lot to do. For most people interoperability means the ability to define a virtual server image or a Java application in such a way that it can be ported to another vendors cloud platform without much modification or difficulty.[143] This 'data image' portability is a tall order and a long way off. But there are other elements of the service that will also need standardization and should prove achievable on shorter timescales: Management API's will need to be developed which can 'talk' between multiple cloud environments[144] as well as traditional issues of application connectivity and integration.[145]

The *Distributed Management Task Force (DMTF)* is addressing the need for open management standards for cloud computing via the 'Open Cloud Standards Incubator[146] which will focus on developing management protocols and security mechanisms to facilitate operations between private, public, or hybrid clouds. The current incubator board consists of AMD, Cisco, Citrix, EMC, HP, IBM, Intel, Microsoft, Novell, Red Hat, Savvis, Sun Microsystems, and Vmware all major cloud computing vendors.

4.7 Jurisdiction and Information Security

We can return to our discussion on Jurisdiction[147] in this final chapter with a better understanding of cloud computing as an IT service delivery tool and better understanding of the relevance and maturity of the current standards framework. We can now more effectively guage the security implications that result from issues of jurisdiction and comment on the effectiveness of current mitigation measures and future developments.

---

[141] http://www.dmtf.org/news/pr/2009/4/dmtf-develop-standards-managing-cloud-computing-environment
[142] Ibid
[143] For example the DMTF's Open Virtualization Format (OVF) standard defines a format for virtual machines in terms that can be interpreted by a variety of virtualization platforms, such as VMWare's vSphere and RedHat's KVM distribution.

[144] Examples are *Amazon Web Services APIs* and *GoGrid's*

[145] The traditional standards in this aspect are things like SOAP, REST and DNS but developments are afoot by companies such as Boomi and Cast Iron which leverage the Internet as a sort of 'enterprise service bus' to facilitate distributed enterprise computing.

[146] See note 125
[147] See section Chapter 1 section 1.2.3 for preliminary discussion.

The UK Data Protection Act requires organisations to control where information is not only stored but also where it is accessed from and which jurisdictions it passes in transit.[148] In distributed cloud environments data may be moved around to gain advantages in availability and processing speed but we have shown that the CSP and customer must ensure the national laws of the territory in which data physically resides adequately protects the rights of data subjects as required by EU privacy laws. The mechanisms in place which allow the transfer of personal data outside of the EEA, such as US Safe Harbor Agreement,[149] may expose that data to localised legal access rights.

Problem: Let's examine a not uncommon cloud computing scenario where a UK based company exports data to servers stored in a datacentre in the US. The Safe Harbor agreement is supposed to ensure that data transferred to a US datacentre from the UK will be guaranteed an 'adequate level of security' in line with the provisions of the EU directive.[150] Some service providers also purport to offer Safe Harbor Data centres where these are located in other countries but uphold UK/European standards of security.[151] This all sounds very promising but in America we also have the Patriot Act[152] and Homeland Security Act[153] both of which may require the CSP to allow the US government access to data held in servers anywhere on American soil. Even within the US itself issues of jurisdiction are important considerations for law enforcement and government agencies and define boundaries for exercising authority. This variance can create problems when issuing subpoenas for document seizure etc in response to a criminal investigation. It is unlikely that the requirements of UK data protection legislation would be placed above these Acts. For cloud customers who may have core information relating to their business activities and personnel stored in the cloud this is not just a moot point but a real tangible business risk. For these customers Safe Harbor seems to be a lowering of the bar from the European national provisions. Especially in light of recent developments in the

---

[148] This was discussed in sections 2.1.1 and 2.1.2

[149] A good summary of the agreement can be found here:
http://itlaw.wikia.com/wiki/U.S.-EU_Safe_Harbor_Framework

[150] General decisions regarding adequacy are made at a community level. Article 29 establishes a working party which is empowered via Article 31 of the Data Protection Directive (Directive 95/46/EC) to insist on legal measures to prevent data transfers to countries deemed to have inadequate data protection legislation.

[151] This approach is suggested by Charles Oppenheim in his book "*The Legal and Regulatory Environment for Electronic Information*." However this approach is unlikely to take hold as it is contrary to the business model of cloud computing which is to make best use of under-utilised resources.

[152] http://epic.org/privacy/terrorism/hr3162.html
[153] http://www.theorator.com/bills108/s1906.html

'German Constitutional Court on the Right in Confidentiality and Integrity of Information Technology Systems.'[154] Here the main impetus of the ruling has been to increase the protection of citizens with the development of a 'new fundamental right' to protect privacy.[155]

Solution: Lack of global standards on information security and inconsistencies in privacy legislation in Europe and abroad mean that the organisation intent on moving critical business activity to the cloud must take what measures are available to secure his data. It is not a prudent approach to leave it to the cloud provider. Use of encryption technology backed up by contractual provision can go some way to alleviating the problems we have encountered. We have introduced these ideas earlier[156] but develop them further now.

The technical details of cryptographic systems[157] are outwith the scope of this analysis but it is sufficient to say that cryptography is not the silver bullet for security problems in the cloud that some people would have you believe. Technologically, information storage and information processing are two different things even if legally they both may be perceived as processing. Encryption can bring real benefit for data storage. Data encrypted by a tried and tested mechanism will provide the required 'adequate' security provided that this is also accompanied by 'adequate' security process and policy to ensure the encryption keys, or significant key material (passwords etc) are not easily obtained by persons not authorised to view the data. Many of the issues of jurisdiction relating to data privacy then do become less pressing as without the encryption keys, and assuming a well designed crypto system,[158] the data cannot be viewed. However data can still be made unavailable through technical failures or theft and where technical processing is required it must first be decrypted.[159]

---

[154] W Abel and B Schafer, "The German Constitutional Court on the Right in Confidentiality and Integrity of Information Technology Systems – a case report on BVerfG, NJW 2008, 822", (2009) 6:1 *SCRIPTed* 106, http://www.law.ed.ac.uk/ahrc/script-ed/vol6-1/abel.asp

[155] Ibid

[156] In Chapter 1 (1.2.1) we outlined the skeleton of a cloud computing contract and in Chapter 2 (2.4) we considered the strengths and weaknesses of using encryption to secure data in the cloud.

[157] Encryption does not just involve a strong, mathematically hard to break algorithm such as AES 256 (symmetric data encryption algorithm) but also requires elaborate key exchange, authentication and authorisation, non repudiation and identity management methods to develop a secure 'cryptographic system'. The implementation of these systems can be subject to flaws which present vulnerabilities which can be exploited by criminals.

[158] Details on standards for development of cryptographic systems can be found here: http://www.oecd.org/document/11/0,2340,en_2649_34255_1814731_119820_1_1_1,00.html

[159] There are developments in cryptography that may have potential to allow processing of encrypted data whilst it is encrypted!! IBM has been expending some effort in homomorphic encryption which they say will allow the analysis of data by third parties without revealing the data content. http://www.banktech.com/risk-management/showArticle.jhtml?articleID=218101557

This is where international cloud standards will eventually come into play. At the present time, regardless of whether cloud computing will be subject to specific statutory regulations in the future, current data protection provisions of EU law will apply to cloud computing. As we have mentioned the cloud customer must ensure his data protection requirements are considered binding in his contract with the CSP but we can now be more specific about the nature of the clauses which *must* be negotiated.

4.7.2   Essential Contractual Clauses

The following list is not intended to be exhaustive but it constitutes the essential negotiations which must take place to cater for the anomalies and foibles introduced to the data protection landscape by cloud computing. Inclusion of data handling clauses in a binding contract will go a long way to establishing trust between customer and provider based on a joint assessment of what constitutes reasonable security practice.

1. ***Define the Scope of Processing***

> Guidance for this clause is provided in
>
> *Chapter 1 (1.2.4) Information Ownership in the Cloud,*
>
> *Chapter 2 (2.1.1) Processing and Control,*
>
> *Chapter 3 (3.2.1) Liability in the Supply Chain.*

The customer must insist that the purpose of and type of processing undertaken by the provider is clearly specified. This clause should also provide details of any third parties which are to be used by the provider for aspects of the cloud service. An obligation must be placed on the provider to ensure that the data protection measures agreed between the provider and customer are also binding on the third party.

2. *Data Deletion*

> Guidance for this clause is provided in *Chapter 2 (2.3) Your Data and Contract Termination*

A clause should be created which addresses the requirements for data deletion in keeping with the fifth data protection principle.[160] This principle requires the 'data user' to "*operate some form of policy for monitoring their data holdings and removing items which are no longer of value or relevance to their activities.*"[161] This obligation will fall on the customer and he should ensure that data he has to delete is also deleted by the provider. The clause should include reference to a data handling policy which the provider has agreed to.

3. *Information Security Measures*

> Guidance for this clause is provided in
>
> *Chapter 1 (1.2.5) Data Protection, Responsibility and Accountability*
>
> *Chapter 1 (1.3) Technical Challenges*
>
> *Chapter 2 (2.1.2) What Guarantee for Data Integrity*
>
> *Chapter 2 (2.4) Security through Encryption*

Here the customer should detail *as far as possible* the **organisational**[162] and technical security measures to be undertaken by the provider. This should address issues previously

---

[160] "..personal data processed for any purpose or purposes shall not be kept for longer than is necessary for that purpose or those purposes" DPA 1998 Schedule 1.

[161] Information Technology Law: Fifth Edition, Prof Ian J. Lloyd. Oxford Press.('Duration of Record Keeping' page 114).

[162] Emphasis appears because organisational aspects of security are often ill thought out with the reliance being placed on technical measures. Technical measures without adequate controlling procedure equates to no net gain in security.

discussed such as: degree of provider employee access to customer data, details of provider processing activity (servers used, data mining, geographic location etc), and use of encryption during both transmission and storage of information.

The traditional hosting model leaves security responsibility firmly with the customer. Customers typically keep sensitive information in house and utilise the hosted platform for specific business needs. In the cloud computing world companies will be looking to maintain all business data including sensitive data in the cloud (therefore saving on IT costs). It may prove useful for a provider to develop a 'cloud security policy' covering essential aspects of their cloud service and bring the customers data within the scope of this policy. In such a situation the providers cloud security policy should be declared as part of the contract. This would help to build the required trust needed to ensure cloud computing thrives as a reliable business model.

4. *Jurisdiction and localisation of data*

Guidance for this clause is provided in

Chapter 1 (1.2.3) Jurisdiction and Applicable Law

Chapter 1 (1.2.5) Data Protection, Responsibility and Accountability

Chapter 4 (4.7) Jurisdiction and Information Security.

To ensure compliance with European privacy laws in connection with the export of data to other countries the cloud customer must know where the servers that process and store information reside. In this clause an obligation should be created on the provider not to transfer data to countries not included in the contract without prior consultation with the customer.

5. *Service Level Agreements for Data Handling*

> Guidance for this clause is provided in
>
> *Chapter 1 (1.2.1) Terms and Conditions for Cloud Computing Contracts*
>
> *Chapter 1 (1.2.5) Data Protection, Responsibility and Accountability*
>
> *Chapter 1 (1.4) Trust, Cloud Governance and Standards*
>
> *Chapter 2 (2.3) Your Data and Contract Termination*
>
> *Chapter 3 (3.2.1) Liability in the Supply Chain*

The cloud customer should seek binding service level agreements for availability and recovery of data. A useful approach is to seek service credits from the provider for network outages. Also, the orderly return of data, or migration to an alternative service, when the cloud contract comes to an end needs to be ensured. This requires sufficiently long notice periods for both customer and provider. The mechanisms to be employed during these circumstances, including the form data will be delivered, should be clearly described in the contract.

6. *Audit Rights*

> Guidance for this clause is provided in
>
> *Chapter 1 (1.4) Trust, Cloud Governance and Standards*
>
> *Chapter 2 (2.1.3) Tracking and Auditing Data in the Cloud*
>
> *Chapter 3 (3.4) Compliance and Audit*

Once establishing obligations on the provider the customer must arrange the opportunity to verify that the provider is meeting these obligations. A clause agreeing the customers audit rights should be worked out. To be fully comprehensive this could involve some difficult negotiation. The cloud customer must ensure they can access relevant parts of the providers business to ensure compliance with their industries regulation and standards framework.[163] If some of this requirement is not possible they should look to bring these aspects of the data flow under the protection of the provider security policies as discussed in clause 3 above.

4.8   Chapter Summary

For the future the development of CAMM[164] looks promising and shows the beginnings of a useful governance model which will extend CoBit and other security standards into the cloud allowing control of third party supply chain dependencies. Unfortunately at this moment in time this framework, or any other, remains only a 'work in progress'.

At present, for commercial cloud computing arrangements carefully drafted contractual clauses are the only way to create reasonable security for both the cloud provider and customer and we have shown something of the content required to make these clauses effective. The division of liability arising within the cloud computing model needs to be handled by confidentiality agreements, SLAs, liability and indemnity clauses. These are all necessary in view of the governance gaps resulting from adoption of the cloud model to clarify where responsibility and accountability lie.

---

[163] Audit and information rights may also require arrangements to be made for regulatory authorities to audit the cloud provider.

[164] See note 62

Conclusion

It would appear that within the global environment in which cloud computing operates, the current legal position assigns responsibility for safeguarding data squarely with the cloud customer as the data controller. However a closer look at the legal framework and particularly the direction being taken by the courts in recent cases shows that where information is concerned the issues may not be so clear cut. The technical awareness of the legal system regarding cloud technologies is increasing. The courts are beginning to take a useful, pragmatic and well balanced approach to evaluating the fairness and effectiveness (reasonableness?) of provider T&C's in meeting customer information security requirements and obligations.

The concept of what is reasonable is central to this balance. It is also nothing new. This after all is what corporate diligence is all about. However, achieving this reasonableness now requires real understanding of well known terms such as: vulnerability, threat, risk and exposure within a new technical landscape. In a cloud computing context these terms are frequently used but often with no real understanding of the **new** relationships between the concepts themselves or their relationship to corporate culture and business ethics. Some behaviour may not be illegal but that does not mean it is ethical. Just because something is not illegal does not necessarily make it right.

Throughout our analysis of reasonable security in a cloud computing environment we have encountered this interaction of legal and ethical precedent. If a building burns to the ground as a result of an arsonist attack, destroying all company records and information then the arsonist is only one small piece of the tragedy. The company is responsible for fire-detection, disaster recovery, fire exits, extinguishers, tested evacuation procedures, data backup, off site storage etc. In a cloud computing context a companies *due diligence* must be exercised in such a way as to prevent security breaches (malicious and accidental) and ensure adequate controls exist to mitigate damage when a breach does occur. Analysis of relevant case law has shown the courts will uphold the principle of '*doing the right thing*'. Paying attention to security best practice, showing prudence and responsibility with regards to relative expertise in contract negotiation, acting on data breach notifications and utilisation of measured and fair exclusion clauses are all examples of doing the right thing. On the contrary ignoring best practice without good reason, using superior technological expertise to negotiate unfair contractual terms, ignoring notifications from customers and creation of 100% liability exemption clauses will not be looked on favourably by many court systems. In general it is better to 'do the right thing' than to 'see what you can get away with'.

Cloud service providers should address ethical issues in relation to governance gaps which appear when moving 'to the cloud'. A common question asked by senior management, when a well meaning technical security professional suggests the inclusion of a required operational measure, is "well what really is the risk?" Unfortunately the expertise of most security professionals will not extend to the required disciplines required to adequately answer this question. Although a valid question, this has become a sort of mantra used by management (who often have even less understanding of the issues) to avoid time consuming and possibly costly discussions on an issue which no one seems to have a clear handle on and which from their perspective seems to only show potential for holding up delivery of the already overdue cloud platform. The difficulty in answering the question arises because a big part of the answer lies, to a substantial degree, with the effectiveness of contractual provisions especially those which attempt to limit the provider's liability when things go wrong. This risk is really a risk to a company's ability to contract effectively with its customers. For a service provider, poor governance of cloud security issues equates to poor corporate diligence and a tangible risk to business reputation. This is what *reasonable security* really means. Adoption of operational security measures based on best practice and controlled via existing standards shows prudence in security methodology.

As cloud computing develops risks of identity theft and fraud will feature in more litigation claims. We will likely see increases in the following:

- Claims against cloud providers for poor security measures, loss of customer data and hacking damage.

- Disagreement on provider use of data mining.

- Data breaches in violation of EU national laws implementing Directive 95/46/EC

- In US there are likely to be claims against service providers involving information passed to government organisations and others in violation of Fourth Amendment rights.

- Claims relating to: surveillance, snooping or censorship by service providers.

At the present time, with the absence of mature cloud computing standards, a CSP who proactively addresses the gaps arising from adoption of a cloud computing model by using contractual provision to clarify division of responsibilities and liabilities between themselves and their customers will go a long way to convincing the courts, in any litigation, that they have been reasonable in their approach to doing business.

BIBLIOGRAPHY

Books

Anthony T. Velte, Toby J. Velte and Robert Elsenpeter	Cloud Computing A Practical Approach. ISBN:9780071626941 McGraw-Hill/Osborne © 2010
David G. Hill	Data Protection: Governance, Risk Management, and Compliance. Auerbach Publications © 2010
Harold F. Tipton Micki Krause	Information Security Management Handbook 6th Edition
Thomas J. Smedinghoff	Information Security Law: The Emerging Standard for Corporate Compliance. IT Governance © 2008 ISBN:9781905356669
Eric A. Marks, Bob Lozano	Executives Guide to Cloud Computing. Wiley. ISBN 978-0-470-52172-4.
L Edwards and I Brown	"Data Control and Social Networking: irreconciliable Ideas?" in A Matwyshyn (ed) Harboring Data: Information Security, Law, and the corporation, Stanford Law Books, 2009
Prof Ian J. Lloyd.	Information Technology Law: Fifth Edition. Oxford Press.
Alan Calder	IT Governance (4th Edition): A managers guide to data security and ISO27001/ISO27002.

Charles Oppenheim

The Legal and Regulatory Environment for
Electronic Information **ISBN-10:** 1873699

TRZASKOWSKI, Jan

Cross-Border Law Enforcement in the Information Society (V.
0.82). EU Electronic Commerce Law, Dj0f Publishing, 2004
www.legalriskmanagement.com

Legislation, Statutes and Regulations

EU Directive 95/46/EC

EU Directive 98/48/EC

EU Directive 2000/31/EC

eCommerce Directive (2000/31/EC)

The Electronic Commerce (EC Directive) Regulations 2002 (SI 2002 No. 2013)

30th Council of Europe Conference of Ministers of Justice, Resolution No.3
http://www.coe.int/t/dghl/standardsetting/minjust/mju30/MJU-30%20_2010_%20RESOL%203
%20E%20final.pdf

Directive 96/9/EC of the European Parliament and of the Council of 11 March 1996 on the legal
protection of databases.

Council Directive 93/13/EEC (Annex) on Unfair Terms in Consumer Contracts

Agreement on Trade-Related Aspects of Intellectual Property Rights

The Computer Misuse Act 1990 of UK
http://www.homeoffice.gov.uk/crime/internetcrime/compmisuse.html

UK Regulation of Investigatory Powers Act 2000

USA Patriot Act 2001

Articles and Reports

Simon Bradshaw	Contracts for Clouds: Comparison and Analysis of the Terms and Conditions of Cloud Computing Services. Queen Mary University of London. Paper No. 63/2010
Bossey, Chateau de	'Report of the Working Group on Internet Governance.' June 2005 http://www.wgig.org/docsAVGIGREPORT.pdf
Chris Reed	Information Ownership in the Cloud Queen Mary University of London. Paper No. 63/2010
Burk, Dan L.	'Jurisdiction in a World Without Borders.' Virginia Journal of Law and Technology, 1 VA. J.L. & Tech. University of Virginia, 1997 http://vjolt. student.virginia.edu/graphics/vol 1 /vol 1 art3 .html
Mitchel, Mary.	Role of Open Standards in IT and Telecommunications http://www.mel.nist.gov/div826/msid/sima/interopweek/presentations/openStdsinFed_IT.pdf
Eijk, Nico Van	'Regulating Old Values in the Digital Age.' Legislation and Jurisdiction http://www.osce.org/publications/rfm/2004/12/12239 92 en.pdf

and Roberta J. Morris   of global networks: irrelevance of, goals for, and comments on the current proposals.' Chicago-Kent Law Review [vol. 77:1213 2002]

Gellman, Robert   Privacy in the Clouds:
Risks to Privacy and Confidentiality from Cloud Computing' World Privacy Forum.
http://www.worldprivacyforum.org/pdf/WPF_Cloud_Privacy_Report.pdf

Current Challenges of Developing a Legal: Infrastructure for securing e-commerce.'
http://www.unescap.org/tid/publication/tipub2348_part2v.pdf

Cloud Computing: Benefits, Risks and Recommendations for Information Security ENISA
http://www.coe.int/t/dghl/cooperation/economiccrime/cybercrime/cy-activity-interface-2010/presentations/Outlook/Udo%20Helmbrecht_ENISA_Cloud%20Computing_Outlook.pdf

Article 29 Data Protection Working Party: Opinion 1/2010 'on the concepts of controller and processor.' http://ec.europa.eu/justice/policies/privacy/workinggroup/wpdocs/2010_en.htm

'Information Security Standards and Certifications in Contracting': Information Law Library-
http://www.infolawgroup.com/information-law/

'Field Guidance on New Authorities That Relate to Computer Crime and Electronic Evidence Enacted in the USA Patriot Act of 2001.' Computer Crime and Intellectual Property Section (CCIPS) http://www.cvbercrime.gov/PatriotAct.htm

Towards a cloud-specific Risk Analysis Framework, Siemens IT solutions and services
http://www.it-solutions.siemens.com/b2b/it/en/global/Documents/Publications/CloudSecurity_Whitepaper_PDF_e.pdf

http://www.computerworld.com/s/article/9011459/Have_you_resold_your_data_to_crooks

'Jurisdiction in Cyberspace.' Articles, May 11 2002, 11:06 (UTC+0)
http://neworder.box.sk/newsread_print.php?newsid=4376

http://news.cnet.com/8301-19413_3-20006756-240.html?part=rss
&subj=news&tag=2547-1_3-0-20 : James Urquharts 'Bill of rights'

for cloud computing.

http://cordis.europa.eu/fp7/ict/ssai/docs/cloud-report-final.pdf The
Future of Cloud Computing (European Commission Article).

'Introduction to Cloud Computing Architectures' Sun Microsystems
White paper June 2009
http://www.techrepublic.com/whitepapers/introduction-to-cloud-co
mputing-architecture/1188419

CSA: Cloud Security Alliance, Security Guidance for Critical Areas
of Focus in Cloud Computing V2.1
http://www.cloudsecurityalliance.org/csaguide.pdf

'International Legal Instruments.'
http://www.cybercrimelaw.net/tekster/international agencys.html

Smith, Herbert	'Cloud Computing: key regulatory and contractual issues' Intellectual Property and Technology, and Telecommunications Newsletter. http://www.herbertsmith.com/NR/rdonlyres/044EA5BE-207A-4E6A-9F25-83A2CF00F7EE/16802/IPTMTNewsletterEOctober2010.pd
Grandison, Tyrone	A survey of Trust in Internet Applications: Tyrone Grandison, Morris Sloman. Imperial College, Dept of Computing citeseerx.ist.psu.edu/viewdoc/download
Balboni, Paulo	Cloud Computing Risk Assessment and Security and Resilience in Gov Clouds: ICT Lawyer: www.paolobalboni.eu

Saita, A   Beyond borders: 'Losing the perimeter to gain better data security' 29th July 2004.
http://searchsecurity.techtarget.com/news/article/0,289142,sid14_gci996078,00.html

Lees, John   The Financial Benefits of Cloud Computing.
                          http://www.the-financedirector.com/features/feature61743

http://www.infolawgroup.com/2010/05/articles/information-security-contracts/information-security-standards-and-certifications-in-contracting/#more

http://www.oecd.org/document/11/0,2340,en_2649_34255_1814731_119820_1_1_1,00.html (on cryptographic standards)

http://news.cnet.com/8301-1009_3-10413951-83.html : Amazon EC2 cloud service hit by botnet, outage

http://www.readwriteweb.com/cloud/2010/02/top-5-cloud-outages-of-the-pas.php : Top 5 cloud outages

http://opencloudconsortium.org/ : Test bed for vendor interoperability of cloud platforms

Sun Microsystems white paper on Cloud Computing Architectures.
http://webobjects.cdw.com/webobjects/media/pdf/Sun_CloudComputing.pdf :

"German Court Ruling Threatens Internet Freedom," The Journal For Historical Review, Vol. 19, No.5, Sept/Oct. 2000, at 16. http://www.ihr.org/jhr/vl9/vl9n5pl6 internethtml.

Web Pages

http://opencloudconsortium.org/ : Test bed for vendor interoperability of cloud platforms.

http://www.nist.gov/index.html : National Institute of standards and Technology.

http://www.cloudforum.org/ : Cloud Computing Interoperability Forum.

http://www.dmtf.org/ : Distributed Management Taskforce.

'Internet Law - Jurisdiction.'
http://www.phillipsnizer.com/librarv/topics/jurisdiction.cfm

'Articles and Various Resources on International law.'
http://www.cvbercrimes.net/International/Articles.html

www.microsoft.com/uk/net : Windows azure development environment.

http://developer.android.com/index.html : Android development.

http://www.wto.org/english/tratop_e/trips_e/t_agm0_e.htm : TRIPS Agreement

'Documents on International Telecommunication Union: World Summit on the Information Society, Geneva 2003-Tunis 2005.' http://www.itu.in1/osg/spu/wsis-themes/confidence and securitv/cvbercrime.html

'Internet Law and Policy Forum.' http://www.ilpf.org

'Jurisdiction.' Global Internet Policy Initiative: A Joint Project of the Center for Democracy and Technology & Internews. http://www.internetpolicy.net/jurisdiction/

'Learning Cyberlaw in Cyberspace.' http://www.cyberspacelaw.org/index.html

'The Internet & Law & jurisdiction.' http://users.aber.ac.uk/uuk/lawandinternetsites.html

Appendix 1: Vendor Questionnaire

Questionnaire.

Section 1: Legal and Regulatory

- Do your contractual terms specify a standard of care that you, the provider, must meet with regards to the protection of data?

- Do you use a 'click wrap' approach to contract negotiation on your hosting platform?

- Do you use 'model agreements' to deal with data protection issues in your contractual clauses?

- What contractual provisions do you agree to regarding uptime, if any? Do you provide any type of uptime warranty? If such a warranty exists is it subject to a limited remedy? (If remedies are severely limited, the provider may be shielded from liability).

- Most providers are savvy enough to disclaim any interest in customer data and will freely say that "your data is your data." Well, that's good, but what provisions do you agree to for physically restoring data back at the end of the contract or if you, the provider, is no longer able to supply the service?

- Do you clarify, contractually, the specified conditions and agreed security levels for data storage? This could be important for regulatory reasons, but also for reasons associated with meeting general customer confidentiality obligations or complying with privacy policies.

- Do you attempt to clarify jurisdiction for any disputes within the contractual obligations?

- Do your contractual terms (standard form) deal with assisting a customer to transition to a new vendor or back to a self-managed platform?

- Are standard form contracts used at all?

- Do you use service level agreements (SLA) to handle the security obligations of the cloud provider?

Section 2: Compliance and Governance

No best practice or standards yet exist specifically for cloud computing. These questions are designed to ascertain how an organisation intends to create 'best practice' when assuring effective security measures and operational control in a cloud environment.

- Do you produce audit assertions using an industry standard format such as Cloud Audit A6, CloudTrust, and SCAP etc?

- Do you allow customers to view audit reports?

- Do you perform network penetration testing, vulnerability assessment etc on behalf of customers with documented results and improvement actions (as per industry best practice)?

- Do you perform application penetration tests with documented results and improvement actions?

- Do you allow customers to do this security testing and if not do you advise on the governance gap that results in security best practice.

- Do you conduct internal and external audits regularly which follow a respected audit standard? If yes, what standard do you benchmark against?

- Do your contracts allow audit capabilities for your customers, i.e. physical access to inspect a data center's physical security measures etc?

- Do you have the ability to logically segment data so that in the event of a court order requiring forensic analysis of a customer's data no other customer's data is accessed?

- Do you have the ability to logically segment and recover data for a particular customer so that no other customer's data is affected?

- Do you have policies and procedures in place (documented) which explain how you will protect customer's intellectual property?

- Is the utilization of tenant services mined in anyway for the benefit of the service provider are there 'opt out's' available for the tenants and how are tenants intellectual property rights maintained?

- Can you provide the physical location/geography of storage of a tenant's data upon request?

- Do you allow tenants to define acceptable geographical locations for data routing or resource instantiation?

- Do you have a documented procedure for responding to requests for tenant data from governments or third parties?

- Do you support secure deletion (ex. degaussing / cryptographic wiping) of archived data as determined by the tenant?

- Do you have the ability to sanitize all computing resources of tenant data once a customer has exited your environment?

- Do you provide tenants with documentation describing your Information Security Management Program?

- Do you have documented information security baselines for every component of your infrastructure (e.g Hypervisors, operating systems, routers, DNS servers, etc?)

- Do you have a capability to continuously monitor and report the compliance of your infrastructure against your information security baselines?

- Are administrators and data stewards properly educated on their legal responsibilities with regard to security and data integrity?

- Do you encrypt tenant data at rest (on disk/storage) within your environment?

- Do you leverage encryption to protect data and virtual machine images during transport across and between networks and hypervisor instances? I.E data that is 'in the cloud' as such.

- Does your incident response plan comply with industry standards for legally admissible chain-of-custody management processes & controls?

- Are you capable of supporting litigation holds (freeze of data from a specific point in time) for a specific tenant without freezing other tenant data?

- Do you have a capability to detect attacks which target the virtual infrastructure directly (ex. shimming, Blue Pill, Hyperjumping, etc.)?

- Do you select and monitor outsourced providers in compliance with laws in the country where the data is processed and stored and transmitted?

- Do you select and monitor outsourced providers in compliance with laws in the country where the data originates?

- Does legal counsel review all third party agreements?

- Do you provide tenants with documentation which describes your production change management procedures and their roles/rights/responsibilities within it?

- Do you provide multi-failure disaster recovery capability?

- Do you provide the tenant the ability to declare a "disaster"?

- Do you provide a tenant triggered failover option?

- Do you have controls in place to ensure that standards of quality are being met for all software development?

- Do you have controls in place to detect source code security defects for any outsourced software development activities?

- Do you provide tenants with geographically resilient hosting options?

Section 3: Operational standards

- Have you worked with NIST in developing standards for IaaS especially around:

  1. VM image distribution (DMTF OVF)

  2. VM provisioning and control.

  3. Inter cloud VM exchange

  4. VM SLAs (uptime, resource guarantee's, redundancy)

  5. Secure VM configuration (SCAP)

  6. Persistent storage standards.

- Do you provide a capability to identify virtual machines and/or hardware via policy tags/metadata (ex. Tags can be used to limit guest operating systems from booting/instantiating/transporting data in the wrong country, etc.?).

- For your IaaS offering, do you provide tenants with guidance on how to create suitable production and test environments?

- For your IaaS offering, do you provide customers with guidance on how to create a layered security architecture equivalence using your virtualized solution?

- Data center redundancy and resilience will be paramount in protecting cloud services. The uptime institute has advised that 70% of database outages can be accrued to human error. (Julian Kudritzki, vice president, Uptime Institute). With the move to virtualization even more scope for sizable outages affecting multiple customers will exist. Is your organization acknowledging this challenge by developing stringent management process for the virtualized platform and importantly developing strategies for enforcement of these processes?

www.ingramcontent.com/pod-product-compliance
Lightning Source LLC
Chambersburg PA
CBHW081057170526
45166CB00006B/2092